Takhli Tales —
and other stories

Billy R. Sparks,
Lt. Col. Ret. US Air Force

COVER PHOTO

Captain Billy R. Sparks (left), pilot and Major Carlo
Lombardo (right), electronic warfare officer of the
355th Tactical Fighter Wing, Takhli 1967.

ᴊarks

ISBN: 1481976036
ISBN-13: 978-1481976039

DEDICATION

This book is dedicated to my wonderful family for their love and support through the years. It is also dedicated to the members of my unit for standing beside me and helping me survive to tell these tales.

EDITOR'S NOTE:

I am honored to have helped pull together this collection of Sparky's stories. Over the years of our friendship, I've heard many of them first hand at dinner parties and family gatherings. Never did I fully realize the breadth and depth of his dedication, decoration and exemplary service to our great country.

In editing these pages, I have learned so much about a man whom I am proud to call my friend. His generosity, bravery, sacrifice and spirit will always have a special place in my heart.

E. L. Kaminsky

AUTHOR'S NOTE:

I have written these stories for my family and friends to allow them a glimpse of what I faced during the most significant and most stressful period of my life. Being a Weasel at Takhli was, in my opinion, the single most important thing I have ever done. The mission was demanding, dangerous, and those of us there performed at a level I have never seen before. I doubt that it could be surpassed anytime or anywhere since then.

During my time at Takhli, I performed my duties, often with the feeling that the decisions coming down from above made no sense. Missions like Rolling Thunder (1965 to 1969) served to wipe out over 50% of my aircraft, the F-105, and to kill or imprison a very large number of my friends. I am haunted by the losses that I watched and participated in. My fear is that what I have written may sound like the meanderings of a braggart or the bragging of an egotist. It is my hope that the stories are meaningful and provide some insight into the man I've become.

I write the way I speak, very straightforward and, I think, simply. As far as I know, all of the tales included in this collection are true, or at least as true as my memory allows. Thank you for reading.

Billy R. Sparks,

Once a Thud Driver, aka Barracuda

Lt. Col. Ret. US Air Force

BILLY R. SPARKS, US AIR FORCE ASSIGNMENTS:

Spangdahlem, 49TFW 8TFS, '59/63, F-100 and F-105

McConnell, 23TFW, 563TFS/560TFS '63/67, F-105

TDY to Takhli Apr/Aug '65, 63 Combat sorties

F-105 FWIC, Top Gun '66

F-105 Wild Weasel School '67

Takhli, 355TFW, 357TFS, May/Dec '67

Wild Weasel Flight CC, 77 Combat sorties.

D Flight CC, 5 combat sorties

One landing, zero takeoffs CH-53-E, ½ combat sorties Nov 5, '67.

Nellis, '68/'69' F-105 Fighter Weapons School Instructor & Chief of F-105 Academics for both the FWS & Wild Weasels- F-105

Toronto, Canadian Forces Staff College, '69/'70

Baden Solingen, Germany '70/'72 Exchange Officer, 4Wing, 421 Squadron, A flight CC and Ops Officer- CF-104

Nellis, '72/74 FWIC Chief Of Academics & TFWC Chief of Air-To-Air Tests – F-4D/E

Kunsan, 8TFW, 35TFSCC, '74/75 F-4D & Deputy Base CC.

Nellis, '75/77 AIMVAL/ACEVAL JTF, Test Plans, Test Control, & Test Scheduling,

Retired Nov '77 Lt. Col.

750 Hrs. F-100

2250 Hrs F-105

450 Hrs. F-104

350 Hrs. F-4

4000 Hrs total

145 Combat sorties, F-105 & 1/2 sortie CH3-E (Rescued)

Decorations include- Silver Star w/2 Oak Leaf Clusters, Distinguished Flying Cross w/6 Oak Leaf Clusters, Air Medal w/14 Oak Leaf Clusters, Purple Heart

TAKHLI TIMELINE OF EVENTS

Takhli Royal Thai Air Force Base is a Royal Thai Air Force facility, located in Central Thailand, approximately 144 miles (240 km) northwest of Bangkok in Takhli district, Nakhon Sawan Province, near the city of Nakhon Sawan.

In May 1964 Takhli became a forward deployment location for rotational F-105 Thunderchief squadrons, when the 36th Tactical Fighter Squadron (8th TFW), was deployed to Takhli from Itazuke AB, Japan between May 1964-June 1964. The squadron again deployed to Takhli between 26 August–28 October 1965 (6441st TFW). Another PACAF squadron, the 80th Tactical Fighter Squadron, deployed to Takhli between 27 June–26 August 1965 from the 6441st TFW, at Yokota AB, Japan.

Tactical Air Command began deploying squadrons of the Thud in March 1965 as follows:

563d Tactical Fighter Squadron (23d TFW, McConnell AFB), March 1965-August 1965

562d Tactical Fighter Squadron (23d TFW,

McConnell AFB), August 1965-Dec 1965

334th Tactical Fighter Squadron (4th TFW, Seymour Johnson AFB), August 1965-February 1966

335th Tactical Fighter Squadron (4th TFW, Seymour Johnson AFB), November 1965-December 1966

In May 1965 the 6441st TFW (Provisional) became the host unit at Takhli. On 8 July 1965 the 6235th Tactical Fighter Wing was activated to replace the 6441st TFW.

The F-105 was destined to become a major participant in the war in Vietnam, and the primary aircraft flown from Takhli during the Vietnam War. The permanent assignment of the 355th Tactical Fighter Wing to Takhli in December 1965 ended the temporary squadron rotations from CONUS TAC bases.

355th Tactical Fighter Wing

4th TFW F-105Ds at Takhli in 1965

F-105Ds from the 334th TFS at Takhli, 1966

On 8 November 1965 the 355th Tactical Fighter Wing made a permanent change of station (PCS) from McConnell AFB to Takhli without personnel or equipment as the host unit at the base. The provisional 6235th TFW was inactivated and the equipment and personnel at Takhli were absorbed into the new wing structure. Previously, all of the 355th's squadrons at McConnell had been deployed to various bases in Southeast Asia, two of which were reassigned to Takhli (357th, 354th TFS) and brought back under its control. Squadrons of the 355th were:

333d Tactical Fighter Squadron: 8 December 1965 - 15 October 1970 F-105D/F (Tail Code: RK) (Reassigned from 4485th Composite Wing, Eglin AFB, Florida.)

354th Tactical Fighter Squadron: 28 November 1965 - 10 December 1970 F-105D/F (Tail Code: RM) (Reassigned from 8th TFW, Kadena AB, Okinawa)

357th Tactical Fighter Squadron: 29 January 1966 - 10 December 1970 F-105D/F/G (Tail Code: RU) (Reassigned from 6234th TFW, Korat RTAFB)

The following rotational TDY squadrons transferred their aircraft to the newly-assigned permanent squadrons at Takhli

334th Tactical Fighter: 2 September 1965 - 5 February 1966 F-105D/F)

Temporarily attached from 4th TFW, Seymour Johnson AFB, North Carolina

Inactivated in place, 5 February 1966, aircraft reassigned to 354th TFS.

335th Tactical Fighter: 6 November 1965 - 8 December 1965 F-105D/F)

Temporarily attached from 6441st TFW, Yokota AB, Japan.

Inactivated in place, 8 December 1965, aircraft reassigned to 333d TFS.

Operation Rolling Thunder

Under Operation Rolling Thunder IV in 1966, Thuds from Takhli took a big role in bombing closer than ever before to downtown Hanoi, in an attack on a petroleum-oillubricants (POL) storage facility four miles from the center of Downtown. Ninety-five percent of the tank farm was destroyed, and the smoke column from burning fuel rose to 35,000 feet. As icing on a successful mission, 18 trucks were destroyed by 20mm Vulcan cannon strafing after the bombing, and one MiG was shot down.

The 355th TFW participated in major strikes against North Vietnamese logistical areas. Among the targets hit by   the 355th were the

Yen Bay Arsenal and storage complex, Viet Tri Railroad and highway bridge, Hanoi petroleum storage complex, Dap Cau railroad and highway bridge, Phuc Yen petroleum storage and Thai Nguyen railroad station and yard. In May 1967, the 355th TFW received its first Presidential Unit Citation for action from 1 January 1966 to 10 October 1966.

During this time, the wing flew 11,892 sorties, downed 2 MiGs, and damaged 8 more. Although the F-105 was not designed to be primarily a dogfighter, the aircraft was successful in killing at least 27 confirmed North Vietnamese MiGs in aerial combat.

On 11 August 1967, the 355th conducted a raid on the Hanoi railroad and highway bridge. Thirty-six strike aircraft led by the 355th dropped 94 tons of bombs and destroyed one rail span and two highway spans on the northeast side of the bridge. The superstructure was damaged and the highway portion on the north side of the bridge, where it crossed the island in the river, was cut. This stopped the movement of an average of 26 trains per day with an estimated capacity of 5,950 short tons. Two aircraft were damaged, but no pilots were lost. The heart of the North Vietnamese transportation system had been dealt a severe blow.

On 8 October 1967, a flight of F-105's from the 355th TFW attacked and destroyed, on the ground, 2 Mil Mi-6 and 4 Mil Mi-4 Soviet built helicopters. On 24 October, The 355th lead a strike against the Phuc Yen airfield 18 miles north of Hanoi and the largest in North Vietnam. The airfield, which had been untouched prior to the raid, was left unserviceable. On 14 December, under heavy anti aircraft fire, the Wing attacked the Paul Doumer bridge, a vital link between Hanoi and Red China. For the third time, the bridge comes down.

In July, the 355th TFW received its record 3rd Presidential Unit Citation for action from 12 April 1968 through 30 April 1969. During this time frame, the wing dropped 32,000 tons of ordnance on 2,100 targets while flying 17,000 combat sorties.

Source:

http://en.wikipedia.org/wiki/Takhli_Royal_Thai_Air_Force_Base

Wild Weasels

The first "Wild Weasel" aircraft came to Takhli in 1966. The Wild Weasel concept was originally proposed in 1965 as a method of countering the increasing North Vietnamese SAM threat, using   volunteer crews. The

mission of the Wild Weasels was to eliminate
Communist Surface to Air Missile sites in
North Vietnam.

This nickname refers to a mission which was
carried out by a number of different aircraft
types over the years. The first at Takhli were F-
100 Super Sabres, which like all Wild Weasels
had the unique job of baiting surface-to-air
missile (SAM) sites to fire at them. Then "all"
they had to do was evade the missile and lead
an attack on the radar facility that guided the
SAMs. Sometimes they, or the strike aircraft
with them, would fire a radar-seeking AGM-45
Shrike missile which followed the SAM site's
radar beam right back down to the transmitting
antenna. When these relatively early-technology
missiles missed - as often happened - or when
the aircraft ran out of missiles, Wild Weasels
would attack SAM sites with bombs or their M-
61A1 20mm Vulcan cannon.

The F-105G was the designation given to Wild
Weasel F-105Fs which were fitted with greatly
improved avionics. The designation EF-105F
was temporarily applied to these aircraft, but
their designation was eventually changed to F-
105G. The first F-105Gs went to the 357th
TFS at Tahkli RTAFB during the second half
of 1967. The Electronic Warfare Officer
(EWO) in an F-105G (also known as the

"back-seater;" "GIB," for guy-in-back; or "Bear," for trained bear) ran all the new electronic equipment for locating SAM or anti-aircraft artillery (AAA) radars, warning of SAM launches, and sending Shrike missiles down the radar beams.

The 12th Tactical Fighter squadron of the 18th Tactical Fighter Wing, which had been detached to Korat RTAFB from Okinawa, was also equipped with the F-105G and was temporarily reassigned to Takhli in June 1967. A third Wild Weasel squadron, the 44th TFS was reassigned to the 355th from Korat when the decision was made in October 1969 to make the 388th TFW at Korat an all F-4 wing.

The Detachment from the 12th TFS returned to its main unit at Korat and the 44th TFS was returned to Korat in September 1970 from the 355th TFW to the 388th TFW when the decision was made to consolidate the units of the Wild Weasel mission.

Source:

CHAPTER ONE

BILLY REID SPARKS
BACKGROUND

Everyone starts somewhere and for me it was way too early in the morning of December 7, 1934, a few miles west of Hardyville, in Hart County, Kentucky. My Father was Coy Reid Sparks and my Mother was Kathleen Sparks, nee McDonald. I was born at my Grandparent's, Gene Weeden and Ruth Sparks. Since my Great-grandfather was named John Wesley Sparks, you may assume that we were not Catholic.

According to family myth, the first Sparks landed at Jamestown, Virginia Colony in 1628 from a debtor's ship. He promptly jumped bond and disappeared in the hills - setting an exemplary precedent for following generations of Sparks. My antecedents reached Kentucky with the second Boone party and remained there. My Mother's family was originally Clan McDonald of the McDonalds of the Isles, noted cattle thieves. They came from Scotland to Northern Ireland with the Lord Protector, and left for the Colonies in 1748. Small shopkeepers, they have been living in Kentucky nearly as long as the Sparks. I was issued as Billy Reid Sparks - there was a Circuit Rider/Preacher named Coy Reid, Dad was named for him and the same middle moniker was passed to me.

My parents were married in 1927, and like many in America suffered through the depression. My parents were about as different as any two people can be. Dad was quiet, unassuming, and almost shy. Kathleen was anything but quiet. She laughed at everything, loved people, was gregarious, an outgoing. Kathleen McDonald was the youngest of eight children and dropped out of school in the 8th grade to take care of her mother after she was diagnosed with breast cancer.

Her father, Benjamin Granville McDonald, owed a country store in Hardyville and, to shut Kathleen up, bought her a Model T when she was 16 as partial payment for having cared for her mother and an his brother who was dying of 'Consumption'. Dad was the older of two boys from a very poor farm family and a real Jock, all state Basketball and Baseball. Both my parents played on their High School Basketball teams. Dad was an all state center at 6' and could jump vertically and hit the rim with his elbow. Memorial, their school, only had 10 boys total, but they managed to make it to the State Finals in Louisville.

They eloped in Apr '27 when Kathleen was 20 and Coy Reid was 16. Mother was boisterous, funny, and gregarious. Dad was quiet, unassuming, and shy.

They stayed married until my Mother died at 91 after they had celebrated their 70th Anniversary. One of my McDonald Aunts once said that my mother and I spent most of our time embarrassing my dad.

They made it through the worst of the depression better than most because Dad was a baseball pitcher and managed to make enough money in Sunday games to keep us all in bread and beans until he caught on in the minors. They moved from Hart County to Hopkinsville Kentucky, where dad pitched in the minors until '38. Dad also had a series of jobs there in Hardyville, mainly related to account keeping. He worked Tobacco Auctions, Livestock Auctions, and was bookkeeper for the local Sinclair dealer.

We had very little money but didn't notice because everyone else was in more trouble than we were. Dad was an avid hunter and crack shot. He is the only man I've ever seen who could regularly kill five birds on a covey rise, although that was before a three-shot plug was mandatory for shotguns. I was in the fields with him when I was five, and kept at it until I was sixteen.

Eventually, Dad got started in the used car business tow-barring cars from Detroit to Hopkinsville. First with two cars a trip, he got it up to eight by having other guys drive with him in pairs - one car drove and tow-barred another behind it. But later Dad got stuck with eight cars; all running on bad tires when rationing hit in 1941. He needed a new job and was hired by the Henry Vogt Machine Company in Louisville as a machine operator where he stayed for over 30 years.

Our family transplanted to Louisville in March '42. Since my Mother was the eighth child in a family of eight, she concluded that eight in a family was overdoing it, and consequently I was all there was. She did, however, furnish me with a platoon of McDonald cousins, 28 or 29 at last count. Kathleen was an avid reader and read to me constantly. She says she taught me to read when I was 4.

My few memories of that time were very happy. Mother's sister, Mary Peden, lived on a near 600 acre prosperous farm in Christian County near Hopkinsville. My Aunt Mary and Uncle Lucien became a second set of parents to me and their three boys all claim to have raised me in spite of my mother. I started school in '41 and I can vividly remember my 7th Birthday party at the Peden farm, 7 Dec '41. We were having great time until it seemed that everyone became angry. My Uncle Lucien picked me up, hugged me and said "It isn't your fault, it's those damned Japs!"

After we moved to Louisville in early '42, it was mandatory that I spend several weeks on the Peden farm each summer – to avoid becoming a 'City Slicker.' Mother started at Montgomery Ward in the summer of '42 as a clerk and I became a 'latchkey kid'. I was sent for the first of many six-week sessions at the Peden farm that summer. My oldest Peden Cousin was Warren, was called up with the Kentucky Guard in '42 and was given a Battlefield promotion 'D-day. The next Peden Cousin, Donald, dropped out of the

University of Kentucky and went into Air Corp pilot training for B-24s. He made it through a tour in B-24's in Europe and survived 5 trips to Ploiesti including the infamous first low level raid. My Cousin Joe, five years older than I, was left to raise me. I was most happy to be able to spend some time with Warren and Don in '46.

My parents moved every time the rent came due for the first three years in Louisville - until we bought a place in Highland Park in South Louisville for a whopping $1,750 early '45. Since we didn't stay anywhere very long, I had few friends until we moved to Highland Park. I started school at Mary D. Hill Elementary in a rather shabby neighborhood on 6th Street, but only lived in the district for four months. My Principal, Mrs. Dixon, told Mother that she wouldn't tell anyone if I continued at her school. I went there for the rest of grade school regardless of where we lived. I rode the streetcar to school and became the family expert on the streetcar system. I took all of my rural cousins around Louisville when they came to visit. I was very active, read obnoxious, as a child and had more freedom than anyone I ever met. I read omnivorously and played every game I could find. I managed to skip grades 5-A and 6-B and went to Louisville Junior High the fall of '46.

I certainly was not a City Slicker. I really thought of myself as a farm boy although I had lived in a city for most of my life. I managed to hitch a team of huge draft horses to a dray wagon when I was 8 and they became my team. I drove a pickup and a small

Case tractor in the fields when I was 10. I was 11 before I had enough weight to pull the flywheel of the big John Deere to start it. From then on I was able to drive every thing on the farm including the family sedan. When I was 12, my job was to drive my Aunt anywhere she wanted to go - my time for 'Driving Ms. Mary.' My last year on the Peden Farm was in '48 when I was 13. Joe Peden got very tired of me sticking to him like glue and started me out dating that year. He'd fix me up with a young lady, give me the keys to the pickup, stick a six-pack in cab, hand me a buck, and send me to the drive in. If those girls had ever figured out they were with a 13 year-old, both Joe and I would have been beaten to death.   It was an interesting summer for many reasons. I still miss the old farm house, the big stock barn, all 65 head of dairy cattle, 35 head of White Faces, Tobacco fields, and most of all, the peaceful reassuring life there.

Louisville Schools were segregated by race at all levels and by sex after Junior High. There was only one Junior High within the Louisville City Limits (most of the city was outside the city limits). There was Louisville Girls High that shared the huge building, Halleck Hall, with the junior high. Louisville male High School was the academic High School and Louisville Manual was workplace oriented. I studied Saxophone in the 7th grade and made the Band in the last semester that year. I also studied Clarinet and made the Louisville Girl's Concert band as lead sax, and the Louisville Girl's Concert Orchestra on a Clarinet – needless to say, I was discovering girls early.

The Louisville school system had a system of dividing the students by perceived ability. I was a fair student. The top quartile curriculum went as fast as the teacher could teach and the fourth quartile teachers were left with whips and chairs. I managed to stay in first quartile classes - except when forced into a bottom class due to a scheduling conflict with my music classes. I begged the Principal for help and he did a swap so I could take classes with the year ahead for a semester, and I had to live through the absolute toughest math teacher in the school for an entire year. She had a PHD in math and was a strict disciplinarian. Mrs. Millburn was a formidable woman, and taught me more in one year that I learned in the rest of my life - remembering her now still gets me half-ready to stand at attention.

I grew tall early; reaching 6' by my eleventh birthday. I was all arms and legs with more elbows and knees than most. Being habitually clumsy, I must have been a true pain in the butt in those days. My Mother and Father both were athletic when young, but I was noticeably gawky and clumsy. My dad loved to teach young pitchers and often had a couple of likely prospects around to be helped. I was 18 before I could throw a curve. I was also clearly inept at pitching and fielding. As a last resort, he tried me out as a catcher and I was able to do that. I improved my skills and from then on was a catcher. Only when everyone else was toes-up in a sickbed was I allowed to be a first baseman. Dad taught me a lot about catching and I caught for all of his young student 'phenoms'.

One of the best was a tall, wild right-hander named Bobby Basham. Bobby could really bring the heat! He had a signing bonus with Cleveland for $35,000, but needed help. I caught him almost a year - sometimes actually with the glove instead of my body. He was wilder than a baseball machine shooting golf balls. I wound up getting my body in front of his pitches to grab the rebounds! He lasted one and a half seasons in the minors until he was advanced to his level of incompetence - where batters could hit fast balls. He returned home, but with $35,000 - which was four houses in 1948.

Dad decided to relocate again from Highland Park to a small twenty-acre farm in southern Indiana. We moved in the spring of '48. Dad daily drove to work at 6:00 AM, and I would walk to school and back to where he worked for a ride home when he got off at 4:30 PM. It played hell with what I then considered my social life. In the summer of '48 I got a nifty job digging post holes for zero dollars per week fencing the 20 acres into two large fields and three smaller lots. Added up, the holes seemed to equal a tunnel halfway to China. The job did a memorable job on my grip and catcher's calluses.

I was 14 when I started my sophomore year at Silver Creek - pronounced 'crick'- in the fall of '48. For the first time I rode a School Bus instead of a street car - I still like trams. I decided to go out for Basketball since Silver Creek had only 250 students including the Junior High and no football team. I was 6' and weighed a skinny 125 pounds. I made junior varsity and learned that 'all men are *not* created equal.' Those big ole' Southern Indiana farm boys were a hell of a lot better equipped to play center/forward than this lad would ever be.

Coach Sailor was a great believer in physical conditioning. He taught me that I could run forever if threatened enough. I practiced until 5:30 PM and then ran another 2 ½ miles after I got dropped at a friend's house. I might have been mediocre on the court, but I was in hardy shape. I made junior varsity - and through weird happenings wound up dressing with the varsity.

We were playing Seymour, Indiana. They had a 6'4" center who was as dirty as they get. He was whipping on our center big time, and the Coach sent me as a replacement. He told me to "Get him mad and make him hit you!" I crinkled his toes, pulled his shorts down, and bit him on the belly when we jumped for a rebound. He smacked me in the chops, yelled a few negative compliments, and took a second swing at me. This gave me two penalty shots, and he was booted out of the game. I made them both and then got two more baskets. We won and left Seymour under Police escort – and I was awarded a Varsity Letter. I started to be allowed to drive the family wheels for dates and 'Social Occasions' when I was 15. It did wonders for my ego.

Academically, Silver Creek was taking me nowhere. Every class I had covered before and was bored silly. Mother tried sly tricks to inspire her little boy to no avail. She finally went to New Albany, in another County, about 15 miles away, and asked if I could transfer there. They agreed, and I went to another new school for my last two years. New Albany is on the Ohio River and, then and now, has around 50,000 residents. NAHS, New Albany High School had 1,750 students. My dad would detour through the city and drop me off way early for classes my first semester. I'd either hitchhike home or catch a bus to Henry Vogt and ride home with him.

I was still allowed to drive the family pickup for dates until I was 16 in December and could get my own car and legally drive. I had saved enough for a real clunker, '37 Plymouth that I bought 8 Dec '50. I had been borrowing Dad's car for dates since I was 15.

I had played against the NAHS basketball team and knew better that try out for them. The Bulldogs had lost a total of twelve season games in the last seven years and only lost one when I was there. I was 6' and still weighed a whopping 135 - I knew football was not for me. I could only catch in Baseball but had lost my desire to squat behind a plate and stop fouls with my face. Instead, I happily played in the Marching Band, the Symphony Band, the Pep Band and the Orchestra – having noticed that there are a lot more desirable girls on the band bus than the sports team buses. I also learned in junior high that double-reed players are amazing kissers - even a female trombone picker ain't all that bad either. I learned to dance my Junior year and, after I got the clunker, my social fife picked up a ton.

I met Reid Crosby in band class the first day and we have been good friends ever since. Reid put together a Dixieland/Dance/Jazz band – and asked me to bring my horn and play at a local club with them! I played Sax and Clarinet for the next two years with Crosby's band, averaged a gig per week, and made $10 to $25 per night. I thought I had died and was wandering in heaven! Music paid for my gas and supplied more spending money than I had yet seen. This also helped my social life. Reid introduced me to local musicians, and I got to hear genuine Jazz in bars in Louisville – the ones with bartenders who didn't check the strange IDs of young idiots.

I found a place downtown on 4th street with a very young (twenty) black Piano Picker, Flip Phillips, who was incredibly good. He played Jazz as well as anyone I'd heard. For some reason, he let me sit in with his group and later introduced me to two Jazz bars in the blackest section of Louisville. I was allowed in, once the Jazz pianist introduced me, and tried to get there once a week. I didn't like beer, so I learned to drink Bourbon and Coke, and I was probably the only white dude for a mile in any direction.

Sadly, that wonderfully talented young black piano player was hooked into heroin, and died of an overdose before reaching twenty-two. It made me terrified of all drugs ever since.

The only negative part of New Albany was that they were academically undemanding. I never brought a book home and never studied - and managed to graduate third out of a class of 279. I had a great time playing in the band, in Reid's Dixie group, and managed to date more than a few noticeably comely girls, but with the books I became a full time loafer. I did have a good social life and played every game there was with my buddies.

I met a charming young lady my junior year, Dell Whittinghill, and decided she was the best of the best. However, Reid Crosby charmed her first and she became 'Reid's' girl. From time to time he would make her angry and I was the patsy who 'fixed' things up. This melodrama went on for quite a while. Reid graduated in '51, and since Alumni could not go to Proms, he asked me to take Dell to my senior (her junior) Prom. The dance took place on the Belle of Louisville, a Sternwheeler out of Mark Twain. I happily agreed, and Dell and I had a fine time. I did as I was told, kept her out all night, and even took her to school next morning in her Prom dress. I mentioned to Reid that he should get another patsy because she was looking finer all the time.

I managed to get a tuition-and-books scholarship to the Indiana University Music School before graduation and then spent the summer working at Henry Vogt Machine Company as a laborer. In the spring I went to IU and pledged Sigma Nu, giving me a place to live while I attended. They helped me get a job as a pearl diver - i.e., dishwasher in the Chi Omega Sorority - that provided three meals a day. The scholarship brought me to the music school at Bloomington. First year went fast. I dove for pearls for food, camped out at the fraternity, and discovered that I despised music school.

I loved music and still do. I could play anything written, but could not solo to save my soul. Crosby told me that if he spilled ink on a page, I could sight read it. He also told me that I would choke on a scale when I was asked to put my own heart into it. I played in the Concert Band, Orchestra, and the Marching Hundred and loved it. I even got to march at Eisenhower's Inaugural in '53.

All that aside, the Music School and I were very much not a fit! Most of the students there didn't know who the president was, and many didn't care if there was one. I made it through the year and both Reid Crosby and I were accepted as members of Sigma Nu in the late spring. I became a bridge player, polished my social skills, played on almost every house team and made my grades. Crosby and I rode for the house in the 'Little 500' Bicycle race. There are 33 teams in the 200 lap race with four members each.

We had 'Big' Stoner, our best rider, Al (Young) Stoner, Crosby and me. We started dead last and had very little chance of being in the top 20. I started and sprinted for 6 laps and took us to 15th, Crosby really hauled and we were 9th when Big Stoner took the bike. He broke his leg on his second lap and we were now last. Al was hopeless; so, Crosby and I rode 190 total laps and a 10th place finish. That gave the house seats in the Parquets at the Speedway for the real '500'. I also learned to like crawling around in caves and became a Spelunker for the next 5 years. I was ready for my second year and changed schools to 'Big and Easy' - Business and Economics.

I went back to my summer job at Henry Vogt only to be met by a strike there - as happened at most other companies in the Ohio River valley. For the first time in my life, I couldn't find a job or an income anywhere within 300 miles of Louisville. It meant no school for me in the fall of '53. I rode around with a friend, on leave from the USAF waiting for Cadets in his MG most of the summer, being cool.

In September Crosby volunteered for the draft and went to Wurzburg, Germany, and played there in an Army band for two years. I got a job ditch digging until mid-September '51 when I became a 'Ballistic Technician' at the powder plant in Charleston, Indiana. I avoided getting blown up and saved enough for an easy next year at IU. Just before Reed left for boot camp, he made Dell mad one last time - and I told him I was after her now, big time. His only request was that he be the best man if I could talk her into it. I talked a blue streak, and he was in fact our best man on July 16th, 1955. The big change was that Dell was 'My Girl' and fiancé, when I returned to IU in the fall of '54.

I spent the '54 -'55 year at Sigma Nu house as the boss of the kitchen crew and pledge trainer. The kitchen crew furnished my meals. I still had less than diligent student habits and found that I didn't like Business School any better than Music School. It was too late to switch majors again, or switch Schools, so I looked for something to do. Like many others, I was in ROTC and respected it. I made friends with the Air Force staff who were there mostly to get a degree before retiring. All but one Captain were WWII Bomber crew types who were looking for alternate careers after they hung it up in a few years. The Captain was an F-86 driver trying to stay out of SAC. They invited me out to Bakalar airfield, a small reserve field about forty miles away. They let me land a C-46 the first time I got in the cockpit - and I was hooked!

My second flight was in a C-45 and I ground looped it. I was in dire need of better instruction which they gave me. After that, I finagled an invitation every time I could until the end of the academic year. Other diversions were playing for the fraternity in volleyball and football, catching for the softball team, even swimming. Fortunately, the House won an athletic trophy in spite of my efforts.

I returned once again to Louisville to Henry Vogt and my summer job. Dell and I were married July 16th in New Albany, and moved to Jeffersonville to establish residency in Indiana. Our home was a vintage travel trailer (20' 6" X 7' 4" inside dimension) - a welcome and timely gift from my parents. We immediately moved to Jeffersonville to establish Indiana Residency for in-state tuition reasons

We moved to Bloomington in September where Dell went to work for Bell Telephone. I was a student with a number of random part time jobs. I think I tallied seventy-two during the following two years. We lived on Dell's salary. Tuition, books, food and trailer space rental all came from her $42.50 per week. Our food budget was ten bucks a week. I then weighed 150 and she was wondrously beautiful. I managed to pull in a few dollars a week doing odd jobs - and if all else failed, cooks at Sigma Nu provided leftovers to carry us a while. We were doing reasonably well until the neighborhood squirrels butted in - we had parked under their Black Walnut tree.

They would chomp on walnuts late at night, dropping shells on our metal trailer roof and waking both of us. When young and fully vigorous, and nature knocks on your roof, what should an awakened couple do? We did - and the rabbit died a couple of weeks after the Vernal equinox, Dell's birthday.

I was scheduled to go to ROTC Summer Camp in '56 so I couldn't take my normal summer job. We were squeezed for money far more than usual. The summer of '56 became odd jobs and tending bar before and after the ROTC gig. Our bank account was gasping for air when my senior year started. Rescue came from a former student who had graduated IU on the GI bill. He started a business called Ptomaine Tom's Sandwiches, and I became 'The Sandwich Man.' Carrying a big box filled with sandwiches, milk, and other goodies to Fraternity and Sororities Sunday through Thursday yielded me about $48.00 per week, all cash. My best customers were my Sigma Nu buddies. I'd bring the box, set it up, and a pledge was assigned to peddle the stuff while I played bridge. The fee for handling the box was a 'Big Mother' and a carton of milk.

Dell delivered exactly nine months after her

birthday present; his name is Allen Reid Sparks, thus continuing the Circuit Rider connection. Ptomaine Tom and the big box got me through my senior year, a BS, and my commission as a 2nd Lieutenant.

In June 1957, we went back to Louisville and the job at Henry Vogt - and a new 45' trailer, to park away from walnut trees, while awaiting my pilot training date.

CHAPTER TWO
PILOT TRAINING

I spent the summer of '57 working at Henry Vogt, getting multiple shifts as a time keeper when I was lucky. Double shifts paid time-and-a-half over 40 hours, and double-time over 48. I had two straight weeks of 80 hours, and another three of 60 hours, putting spare bucks under the mattress. Dell had transferred back to Bell Telephone in Louisville, and my mother was like a kid with a new toy all summer, having our new baby boy to spoil. She wanted to spend time with him since he had arrived, but it was too awkward given our pressures of School and work. It would be two more years before she could be with us very long, so she made up for lost time all summer. We decided on a new mobile home when it became likely I would enter the Air Force and go into Pilot Training. We would move twice the first year, and it turned out that we made four moves in two years. Being turtle-like carrying our mobile house with us made sense then - but wore thin as time went on.

Orders for Active Duty and Pilot Training had a go date of 28 September, and a report date at

Lackland AFB of 3 October, I would attend 2ⁿᵈ Lieutenant School for six weeks. About then, the US Geodetic Survey offered a job for six weeks, heading a team dragging supplies up to a moving advance camp for Mammoth/Onyx cave explorers in Central Kentucky. The money was tempting and I thought about it, but Pilot training won easily.

I don't know why they sent me to Lackland for six weeks only to learn how to wear a gold bar - Brown Bars were thought a bit goofy, needing little time to bolster them. The good news was that I was now making $300 plus per month and could afford all the uniforms on the AF list. Dell kept our only clunker car with her in Louisville, and I hitched rides when needed. At the base Club I met Al Logan, and we have been friends ever since.

Orders for Pilot Training came at last and I drew Malden, Missouri. There could be a worse sump hole than the boot heel of Missouri, but fortunately I have not found it. Dell got the trailer hauled down from Louisville and I reserved a parking place at the Base Park. I used a few days in late November to set everything up and tie down the trailer by digging 6' holes and running chains from disc plow blades up to the frame at three locations on each side - thunderstorms out there have a habit of eating Mobile Homes. I began academics the end of November with a Civilian Instructor Pilot, recently forced out in a RIF (Reduction In Force) with fifteen years of service. His name was Earnst; a vindictive tyrant with an attitude a mile long. He disliked almost everyone, and stored his real venom for 2nd Lieutenants - it would be a long six months. He got to me early and often. We were not allowed to wear flight suits off the flight line. The drill was to go to the Gym next to the flight line, change into a flight suit and walk to Ops. We would reverse the process when we left the line. After weeks of being yelled at and cursed at constantly, I developed the need to stop and barf between the Gym and the Ops buildings.

After more weeks of this, I finally decided that he wasn't worth puking for, and I would laugh at the bastard instead - it worked. He'd curse and I'd laugh! It drove the pecker-head scrambling right up his own frustration tree – and saving my sanity and digestion. I finally soloed the T-34 with the first bunch - after being screamed at and cursed as the worst student in the world. I decided this guy was just an incorrigible freak and kept my mouth closed around him. After the T-34 phase ended, I got to crawl up into the T-28 cockpit for the first time and start it. I fell in love with the big, round engines right then. I was one of the first to solo the T-28 - although my maniacal IP never stopped his delirious tirades. I learned early those rudders kept the nose straight ahead – a discovery that became quite handy when I got to Luke AFB and flew the F-100. From the moment I met Earnst, he had yelled at me almost ceaselessly. I can recall exactly two missions without him cursing me out. On those, he said nothing - zip, nada, zero - I conclude that I had therefore flown two perfect sorties. After that, it became a thing with me to outlast the wretch, and I eventually became the only one of the four at our table that hung in the full six months..

Malden weather was less than good most of the time. When we were first sent out solo, there was a real problem finding cloud-free airspace. A classmate finally figured out the cloud cover was actually thin, and zoomed up through it into a wide blue sky. We all knew how to dial the local radio station on our navigation radios and home in on it. This classmate figured that the cloud deck was only a few hundred feet thick and had at least 2500' clear beneath it; so, he got station passage on the Malden commercial radio station, put the T-28 in a spin, and recovered beneath the clouds – after which it was easy to enter traffic and land. This unauthorized nefarious activity carried on until the owner of the Flying School, Mr. Anderson, was up one day with a student and saw a T-28 spin out of the clouds, recover, and enter the pattern for landing. To say that it startled him was an understatement! Anderson followed the Student Pilot down and interrogated him. When he discovered what was happening he grounded my whole class and called a meeting of all instructors and Base Military Cadre – resentment followed. All students were called in and asked how many were flying above and then spinning down through the weather. Most stood and extensive yelling began. Flying was stopped and we were all assigned a quick, early course instrument flying – giving the habitually outraged Earnst something more to scream about. He personally warned me in his usual dulcet tones: "After me, combat…will…be…easy!" - and became tireless in making it come true.

Later, Mr. Anderson, of Anderson Flying School, gave me an unannounced check-ride for my Mid-Phase Check. He was incredibly nice, didn't curse me once, and marked down right-side checkmarks for everything except Barrel-Rolls which were only 'outstanding.' I had racked up a 97 T-Score that was, I was told, a record. Earnst looked at the marks, screamed at me to get my 'chute and get out to the line.' I walked out after him, and incredibly, he berated me again for making him '*look bad with his boss.*' We did barrel rolls for 30 minutes as he cursed every one. One of his constructive criticisms was "Sparks, you #$%&&*@@, you've got concrete for brains and lead for feet"! He actually made me fly in tennis shoes for a week! Getting to finally shed that malevolent potential psycho could well have been grounds for a week-long base party.

When we started Night Flying, I was ambivalent about it. It was a pain in the rear because we were only allowed to fly straight and level with no acrobatics - but the flip-side was that it was truly awe-inspiring at night. There were many more stars above my canopy than above my house, and all far brighter. I found night landings almost as easy as those in daylight after accomplishing a few. We were taught how to navigate visually at night. I found it easy after learning how to recognize patterns of light. With its huge flotilla of tugs moving up and down stream, the nighttime air view of the Mississippi was absolutely majestic. Flood lights from the tugs beamed across the river and extended for miles. When at last we were allowed to fly solo, it became like Shangri-la. A classmate tried buzzing tugs at night, gear down, turning on landing lights as they drew close. That stopped as soon as the tug turned its arc light back at him – it was massive compared to the aircraft's. We practiced night flying on instruments, and for me it remains easier than daytime. My last solo night flight at Malden was a point-to-point navigation check. Instructors circled the turn points and logged each student as we flew past and gave them a call. Grades were on how efficiently we flew the route. That night was crystal-clear, with city lights visible for miles. I recall feeling great enjoyment on that final flight – part of it possibly because at that same time esteemed Instructor Earnst was undoubtedly circling and cursing over some wretched dog patch in Arkansas.

We graduated from that to general instruments. It was sheer torture back again with Earnst - all those flights were dual, with the student in the back seat under the bag. He would get rancorous and make me slow-fly the T-28 just above stall speed, then move the trim controls back and forth in a pitch, roll and yaw. The worst was slow-flying that big engine with the yaw trim fully wrong. My right leg actually spasmed. Even though I tuned him out and laughed at him like a hyena, I'm convinced Earnst was, in fact, a practicing sadist - he forced me to endure everything he could think of.

On the happier side, one my class mates was comic George Burns (wife was Gracie) who had graduated from North Texas State with a degree in Jazz Band. George loved Jazz and was an excellent Sax Picker. He convinced our Base Commander, Lt Col Tinker Cole, to buy new Selmer musical Instruments for a volunteer base band to use in parades. The boss bought the idea and George formed the Marching Band - and of course, a dance band. We played the club Friday and Saturday nights for food and booze, and also were invited to play at the local Country Club for a wee stipend. We were damned good and fully enjoyed it. Lt. Col. Cole somehow got us old Glenn Miller arrangements - possibly because Tinker Cole punched ivories in our dance band. That was my last stab at musicianship and I loved it.

My efforts tying down our trailer paid off. Thunderstorms come through Malden - and even spawned a few tornados. I had helped all my classmates chain their trailers while an Instructor Pilot stood by laughing at us. The first high winds flipped and crashed his brand new Spartan trailer on end and it became a total loss. None of my classmate's trailers suffered damage.

When spring came, I passed my final check ride and I had made it through Malden. I was quite content to be assigned to Webb AFB for T-33's in Big Spring, Texas. Anyplace was golden without Earnst, although Dell and I did enjoy the friends we had made, and actually learned to like Malden.

We drove to Big Springs, Texas, at a leisurely pace in mid-June 1958, and luckily got there the day our trailer arrived. We did spend a night in a shabby local court waiting to get into Webb AFB trailer park - and next day felt the Texas heat! I went to a local Montgomery Ward and bought a 4,000 CFM swamp cooler and installed it in the trailer. I also bought a Lambretta Motor Scooter so Dell could use the car. My son, Reid, was now eighteen months old and ready to take charge. I convinced him the Scooter was actually his, and I just borrowed it for work. He'd put on my Wellingtons, clomp out to the Scooter, and announce that it was his turn to 'drive'. Standing up with his hands on the handlebars, I'd start it and get us going. He'd hold on and use the throttle while I put my hands under the seat and steered us by shifting my weight. He accepted it as his toy now, and I only could use it for work. We'd go out many evenings with him 'driving' - until I sold the scooter next year at Nellis. The swamp cooler I bought almost blew the windows out of our trailer, but kept humidity low enough to make West Texas summer livable. We were ready for Webb and I was ready for the T-33.

I met my Instructor Pilot, First Lieutenant Al Preyss, my first day at Ops. I was his first student to shepherd through a whole class - he had arrived after the last class started and filled in as an IP. He was a bit over 6', slim, laid back, wore his black hair a bit long, and always seemed to be laughing at something. He was also an excellent airplane driver and instructor pilot, who just happened to have a Masters in Aero from MIT where he had written his thesis on the T-33 – I had hit the IP jackpot. The absolute best news was that he *never, ever,* yelled or cursed – obviously, I had been transferred to heaven. Webb AFB's strange system broke Squadrons into Divisions and divided Divisions into Flights. Squadron CC was a Lt. Colonel; Divisions were commanded by Majors, and the Flights by Captains. My Flight CC, Capt. Curt Westphal, was a Korean War F-86 driver with the handle 'Diamond.' No one seemed to have names, only Call-Signs, Al Preyss was 'Titan.' I don't recall any screaming Instructor Pilots in our flight, all were congenial and relaxed, and taught us to think as well as fly. Things just kept getting better - I had found a home among the best the USAF had at the time. Dell and I were friends with the whole class, and got closer with the guys in my flight. During this period the USAF had too many pilots, even though half of our class washed-out at Malden. Competition got fierce and we dropped more guys at Webb. We ended with a 59% wash-out rate. A few years later a Wing CC was fired for having a 25% rate. By that time, the Air Force badly needed pilots.

I remember Webb with a lot of affection. I learned crucial lessons about basic flying and even more about needing to *think* when you are in the air. IP Titan stressed that only one person was in charge of any aircraft and that was the pilot - FAA and everyone else were only advisors. The pilot has the most information available, and has to make every

26

decision. No one else will ever be there when you need help. That was absolutely the best and most important flying advice I ever received.

Al Preyss took a bit of getting used to. When I started contact flying he would sit quietly back in the pit and periodically offer comments like "Good Progress" or "Way to go." When I really riled him, he worked himself all the way up to "Sparky, you can do better than this, I'm disappointed." Inspiration wise, this sure beat the hell out of "You have concrete for brains you stupid #$@%%$#@". Al also gave me a lesson in beauty. I vividly remember the blue sky day with towering cumulus clouds extending for miles when he had me soar up the face of a cloud, roll inverted at the top, and skim the surface until going into a vertical dive down the back side. We'd fly through holes inside clouds and break out around the crevices - just flat play with them. I never saw a cumulus that didn't tempt me to play after that. If you've never felt as free and happy as I did in those minutes, you remain deprived.

There was one first class jerk in the Check Section, call-sign 'Maytag'- because he washed out so many students. He showed up in Diamond flight when we were nearing the end of the Contact Phase. My first awareness of the guy was when he grabbed me and told me I had a 'No Notice Check' right now - Titan and Diamond were both gone that day. We briefed and went out to fly. He was a screamer and curser that could have made Earnst proud.

We entered the proper area and he began bellowing at me to do a Lazy Eight (Acrobatic maneuver). He grabbed the aircraft away from me at the top of the first high 90 degree Lazy Eight bank point, and screamed that I had lost control, which amazed me, since I was exactly where I should be. It was total Bull Crap. I kept quiet however, did the next part of the maneuver and finished the Eight. He contemptuously told me to try to keep the aircraft under control and do a Cuban Eight.

Halfway through the maneuver the trim control went to a full nose-down position and got stuck. The stick got extremely heavy and I tried to tell him, but he was busy yelling. I completed the Cuban Eight and again he grabbed the stick from me. It must have slipped out of his fist because the bird suddenly went into an extreme negative 'G' nose down push. I grabbed the heavy stick and hauled the bird back to level. He launched new insults and told me to try and fix the problem. Nothing worked - the trim was stuck full nose down. Then he declared an emergency and flew back to land. By now I was rip-shit and verging on a conniption, but I kept my jaw clamped. I sat with my arms crossed so no one would think I was flying, and let him land from the backseat. He dropped the poor T-Bird in from about ten feet so hard I thought the gear would collapse. Titan was on mobile and said "write that one up as a hard landing!' We taxied in - with Maytag still cursing me. When he stopped, I raised the canopy and jumped out before the ladder was up. I grabbed the forms from the Crew Chief.

Maytag asked what I was doing and I said I was writing the bird up for a hard landing. He shouted at me to give him the forms, we had a tussle which I won, and I turned my back on him and finished the write-up. He grabbed the forms away and tried to erase my entry as I walked to a maintenance truck and reported a very hard landing to the Zebra (MSGT) in the truck. Then I left him standing there and headed for Ops and the session I knew would kick me out of pilot training. Maytag followed me in and filled out a Pink Slip (Failing Ride). Al showed up from Mobile Control with Diamond in tow and was mad as a hornet. I had the pink sheet in my hand from Maytag and he was still shouting at me. Diamond got his attention and ordered him out of the building, then called in our Division Major for a chat - I was sent home while they met.

Next day I stood in front of the Squadron CC with my IP, my Flight CC, and my Division CC. The Lt. Col. very quietly reviewed the ruckus and asked if I had anything to add. I mentioned that I was still worried about the hard landing. He smiled, nodded, and said the right main had been replaced, and that he knew I hadn't made that landing since Mobile Control had written the airplane up *because* I had my arms crossed at touchdown. He also informed me that I was up for an Elimination Check Ride the next day with Martini, the other Flight CC in my Division - and I was scared spitless.

The following day Martini flew with me until half-way through the ride and said "Take me home." I thought I was dead meat as we returned to land. He took me in and sat me down in front of Titan and Diamond, told them that I passed easily, and to tear up the Pink Sheet on me. At that point, everyone in the room could see that my blood had finally unfrozen, and we all went to the club bar where Martini cordially accepted several Sparky-supplied Martinis. I never had another problem with Maytag after that fiasco. He was removed from the Check Section, forbidden to fly with Students, and only flew test hops after that. I was damn fortunate to have two men in my corner that had real regard for students and were willing to go the extra mile for one.

We got to Formation lessons and Al hit his stride. We started with two-ship formations with an IP in each. He'd tell me how well I was doing 'considering how rough the lead was'- and other absolute lies. I was, however, the first at our table to solo in formation - and was rewarded by him flying lead from the back seat with me on his wing. He started with wing-overs and then big barrel rolls until I was holding steady. Then he progressed to loops and finished with a full Cloverleaf. I was wrung out like a dish rag, but held position until we came back to the pattern for a pitchout and landing. I was quite proud of myself completing an adventure that was something for a rookie flyer to treasure! We hit the bar and he bought me Martinis for an encore. He did so for each of the others at our table when they soloed. Al was risking his career for our egos and we knew it. The man had rather large cajones. When we progressed to four-ship formations, he did the same thing all over again. On our first flight as a four-ship flight three of us soloed with Titan in the back seat of lead. We did extensive acrobatics, rolls and loops, before he took us back to land and debrief. We debriefed at the Club, he bought the sauce, and told everyone we were the new Thunderbird Team - heady stuff! By this time I had had quite a few flights with Curt Westphal, and respected him just as much as Titan. He quietly gave us insights that tied the training syllabus to *real* flying. He emphasized tactical formations used to patrol for MIGs. I loved flying with him and took his pearls of wisdom with me when I left Webb.

I discovered a new and sterner Al Preyss when Instrument Flying began. He was comprehensively demanding about it, and though he never hollered at me, he was a fierce task master. He impressed on me that instrument flying was the single most vital skill required of any pilot - hard to believe sitting in West Texas under those immense blue skies! He worked on me relentlessly until I could hold every gauge at half the case markings. The Altimeter was marked at 20' intervals, I had 10'. The Airspeed had 2 knot marks, I had 1 knot. I thought he was nuts - but I learned that it was possible to accomplish his strict demands. When I got to Germany, I fully appreciated just what Al had been stressing.

Dell and I enjoyed the camaraderie with my class mates. We spent a lot of enjoyable time at the Officers Club Pool with my son Reid. He was dog paddling at eighteen months, and totally fearless in the water. My buddies tossed him around like a beach ball and all he ever did was laugh. Reid happily enjoyed the attention and became drown-proof from then on. My wife and I love dancing and we got in a lot at the club. It was almost a vacation for her, since she wasn't working anymore - after being penniless students we had enough by then to get comfortable.

We called parties for any excuse. The oldest member of our class, our only Captain, had been a Navigator before Pilot Training. He prided himself on concocting the most dehydrated Martini in the state of Texas. He kept a freezer full of Beefeater gin jugs next to a bucket of ball bearings. He'd pull a jug of 'Featers' from the freezer along with a frozen martini glass, pour in the Gin, dribble 'Vermouth' over the rim - and drop in three frozen ball bearings. The ball bearings beaded the last of the water out of the glass. It made quite a show and tasted darn fair-to-middlin.' We had two Spanish Officers in the class with us. One was a very quiet and austere Captain. The other was a tall and handsome Lieutenant named Rodriquez, who, puzzling to him, immediately became 'Speedy'. We also had three German Students. Klaus Leinert was a Prussian with a lively sense of humor. He was a fine pilot married to a lovely Bavarian Lady named Beth, from Tutzing on Stamberger Zee, near Munich. Wolfgang Grunewald was from Essen, married to a naturally friendly lady, Hildegard - who just happened to be pregnant at the time... The class clown was a Bavarian named Werner Lupertz. Werner was a first-rate artist who did caricatures of all of us. All three got their wings and transferred to Luke AFB from Big Spring.

One thing of lasting importance did happen to us at Webb. Dell and I had discussed adding to our family and had decided to wait until I had my wings and we were at our permanent station - about a year more. Another rabbit died in late June and Dell started to thicken around the waist. She and Hilda delivered almost the same time at the Luke Hospital. I tried to sue Goodyear again, but still had no luck.

The bad part of Big Springs was losing several of my friends to wash-outs, one IU buddy to a broken neck at the pool, and a super guy from Michigan was killed in a T-Bird.

My class had outstanding flying weather and progressed well ahead of schedule. Diamond's Flight led the bunch. We were scheduled to Graduate 28 November, but at our pace, we were going to reach grad requirements in October - six weeks early. We completed all the check rides with six weeks to spare, and eased back to a relaxed flying schedule of three days a week. Extra time offered extra opportunities, so I got myself on a cross country jump to San Francisco. Titan and I flew to Williams, refueled, and then to Hamilton Field north of San Francisco. Al had an uncle in the city who picked us up and took us to dinner at a great German restaurant - and then to the Top of the Mark for drinks and the fog show. The next day we wandered around the 'Ville' and had dinner on the wharf. We even got Lobsters to take home. Al wrapped them tight, sprayed them with a CO2 extinguisher and froze them solid. They were stowed in the nose of our T-Bag and we filed for Kirtland AFB at Albuquerque. He put me in the back seat under the bag and had me climb to max altitude, to keep the Lobsters frozen - and show me what a squirrel the T-33 is at high Altitude. I managed to wobble up to 49,000' which is about as high as you can fly a T-Bag.

But after a while at that altitude, I got a strange tickling feeling that wouldn't go away. My altimeter told me the cockpit was at 42,000', but since the rest of the plane was at 49,000, mask pressurization was not worth much. The mask was blowing my lungs full every breath, due to the pressure breathing level required at that altitude. The sensation grew worse and I told Al. He asked if I had checked for Paresthesia. I remembered the name from class but still can't spell it. I knew it caused nitrogen bubbles forming under the skin, and was dangerous since those bubbles could also form in bone joints and inside the brain. He took over the bird and had me roll back the hood and check my arms for broken blood vessels - I had them. Hearing that, Al got very embarrassed and immediately obtained clearance to descend to a lower altitude. It made us lower on gas and a little anxious about Petrol when we arrived at Albuquerque. I was fine, had no symptoms beyond an arm rash, and finally talked him out of taking me to the hospital. We flew low altitude to Webb and he made me report to the Base Hospital there. The Flight Doc reamed Al's butt after checking my arms and chest, but I was released next morning and arrived home to help Dell fix our first Lobster.

My best flying at Webb came in the last month. I got to go up with Diamond several times, and he started me on Basic Fighter Maneuvers 101 - dog fighting. There was a particular flying zone verboten to students, and the dog fighting performed there was also forbidden to students. Only IP's were authorized to fly in that zone, and hassling anyone there was a definite no-no for students. It was an unofficial bounce area for Instructors where they could unofficially hassle each other in mock dog fights. On the very first day we went into that zone he put me in the front seat and egged me into an attack on an unsuspecting T-33. It was being flown by Martini, who was also a veteran F-86 pilot. With Diamond's coaching, I waxed his rear! Nothing so far had ever given me a kick like that! Diamond took me to the Club - and Martini kept his own gentleman's code and bought the martinis.

I managed to get into the Hassle zone several times after that and racked up a few victories – with, of course, Diamond there to coach me. I began to think my excrement gave off flowery aromas, when Westphal, AKA Diamond, one of the quietest and deadliest birds in our galaxy, gave me a full-course humility lesson by sending me up with Titan and pounding the both of us into fine, pulp-like substances. I bought the rounds of Martinis that night.

One of my last flights with Captain Westphal was an out-and-back to Laredo. We really went there for a load of cheap hooch from his bar. Getting there, he decided to visit a friend and the visit went on until after dark - I believe we wound up somewhere on the south side of the river. I became introduced to numerous tasty concoctions, but made morning light painfully difficult to navigate. I was poured into the T-33's back seat balancing a huge crate of bizarre booze in my lap - the makings of an absorbing ride back to Big Springs.

In early November all of us were called into an auditorium for airplane selection. Class survivors were getting our Wings on the 28th of that month, and it was time to choose where we would spend our beginning careers. Airplane selection was by class standing. The Top Grad got first choice, followed be the next in the standings, until all assignments were filled. When I came in the door, Titan and Diamond took me by the arms and sat me between them. Aircraft types were listed on a board along with the number of assignments available for them. I looked for fighters and saw three F-100's, several F-86's to Williams AFB, several birds for ADC - and that was that. The F-86F's at Williams had no end assignment and would eventually lead to SAC and bombers. Bombers suck, and I didn't want ADC or Training Command. I had hoped for TAC Fighters since I flew at Bakalar. The F-100's were TAC end assignments. I was third in my class and started to smile. The Top

Grad took Helicopters since he had wanted them all his life. Dave Pine (#4 in the standing) actually jumped up and yelled. Charley Summers took the first F-100 and when my name was called, both Diamond and Titan stood and said "Sparky will take F-100's". The Major who was running things smiled and asked again. Titan and Diamond both started to stand again and he told them 'SIT,' and asked me what I wanted. I told him F-100's at Luke - and right then I owned my chance to become a Fighter Pilot.

Dell pinned my Wings on me November 28th. I wore my Silver Tan uniform; the handsomest uniform the USAF ever authorized. Pinks and greens with a Sam Browne Belt were not too shabby, but Silver Tan was the one.

Al Preyss kept track of me until I retired. He became the first guy to go from being an IP in Training Command to go to the Test Pilot School. He retired as a Full Bull running one of the Labs at Wright Patterson. He was quite a man.

Just before Christmas in 1958, Dell, Reid, and I headed for Luke AFB, the F-100, and TAC.

CHAPTER THREE
COMBAT CREW TRAINING - LUKE

Combat Crew Training in the late '50's was designed to produce a Pilot who was qualified for any mission assigned to Tactical Fighters. It included Air-to-Air, Air-to-Ground or conventional weapons, Special Weapons (Nuclear Weapons), and all of the skills to get to and from the US to where we would be needed. The program had been run by Training Command using Tactical Fighter Pilots and was in the process of being shifted to the Tactical Air Command. It was a one year program with about 480 hours per student with the first 6 months at Luke AFB, AZ and the last 6 months at Nellis AFB NV with a stop between at Stead AFB for survival training. Training was in the F-100. Luke had F-100C and F-100-F's, Nellis had both of those and the F-100-D as well. Of the two bases, I think Luke had the better Instructors and the better Maintenance. Our class didn't start until Jan '59; so, I had to beg 4 hours in Dec from the Test Section at Webb. Dell and I arrived in Glendale AZ just before Christmas found a place for our Mobile Home on Glendale Avenue just west of Grand. That gave me a straight shot west to Luke. We even had an Orange tree next to our rental pad. We were ready.

We found that the trailer was 2 days late due to tire problems and had to stay in a motel running up our costs. We then had to pay the towage and extra tire costs from our pocket. We barely had enough to cover that bill. We were dead broke until I managed to find someone at Luke Finance who would allow me to turn in a voucher for the moving costs and get me an advance before I even signed to the base. We were truly hurting until I found that finance officer. We had Hilda and Wolfgang Grunewald join us for a great Christmas dinner and really celebrated the season. The German Students from Webb were all at Luke for a NATO F-84 class that lasted six months. It was old home week for sure. By the first of Jan the F-100 class was in the Phoenix area and I had introduced Dell to Al and Betty Logan that I had met at Lackland. Dell and Betty knew that they both had a problem, when Al and I went out together, we were trouble. That remained a fact for at least the next 20 years.

I tried to live with a car pool for a couple of weeks, so Dell could keep our clunker, but it was a pain. I decided that 5 miles was easy on the Lambretta even if it was a bit cool in Jan at 0500. Our clunker was '53 Packard Caribbean Capri with that big old straight eight gas guzzler. Of course gas was about 20 cents a gallon and nobody cared. The big problem was that we had no air conditioner and leather seats.

Leather is about the hottest thing around in the Arizona sun. I didn't worry, I had the scooter!

When classes started I found that I had landed in the midst of instructors who were real fighter pilots and had all been there and done that. Even the younger guys all had a bunch of fighter time and everyone could really fly the F-100. Our Operations Officer was Louis Braun, AKA Ugga Honk, and who had flown Gliders at Normandy and Market Garden before he transferred to P-47's. He had been to Korea in the F-86 and had flown on Fisher's wing for most of Fishers kills. Louis Braun looked less like a fighter pilot than anyone I had met. He was over weight, had a quiet air and seemed to be half asleep most of the time. He was about the best there was anywhere at the time for Air-to-Air. We had several others almost as good. I had lucked out again to have such a super bunch of guys to teach me.

Before we were allowed to touch a Hun (F-100) we had Instrument School in the T-33. I was not charmed. These were not the same as the birds at Webb; they were the old Gunnery T-33s. They all had a large placket right up the middle of the Instrument panel where the attitude and primary flight instruments should have been. It seemed as though someone had thrown the gauges onto the board and they stayed where they stuck. They were miserable to say the least. Luke Instrument School was a far cry for what I had at Big Spring. We learned things that had to do with old, out of date or unused in the States equipment. It was extremely hard and the IP's were very demanding. I figured out that they were really trying to get us ready for Europe or some other place with lousy Navigational Aids and about zero control. I was right. Al Preyss had done me a bunch of favors that I had not realized. At Luke we worked on the old 'A'/'N' airway procedures because there were still some somewhere. Each radio beacon put out an 'A' or 'N' in Morse code. When you were in the 'beam', on course between each station, you would hear a steady tone. We learned every trick there was to the use of the Coffee Grinder navigation radio that was located very low on the right side of the panel almost at the level of your feet. I worked my butt off learning to do a Manual DF approach that was sure I would never have to use. The radio had an ADF (Auto Direction Finder) capability that allowed a needle to point toward the station. Man DF was used when the signal was very low or masked by the output of a thunderstorm. You had to fly left handed, manually move the antenna back and forth with a switch on the coffee grinder to get the max signal. You were bent over the stick, flying left handed, with your right hand at you're your socks, constantly moving the antenna back and forth to get the best signal and watching the ADF needle, it was a pure bitch! I'm very glad I learned because I was forced to use that technique at Aviano about a year later. The Instrument School was about as much fun as whacking yourself with a hammer, but it sure felt good when we finished and could go and check out in the F-100.

Iceman Stait, the Instructor I was assigned to for

F-100's was just checking out as an IP at Luke; so, I had Philco give me all my early rides in the F-100. He was a senior IP with a batch of time in the F-100 and never raised his voice. Aircraft checkout was a piece of cake. My first three rides were in the F-100F with Philco in the pit and me upfront. It seemed like the biggest thing I had ever seen. Philco never touched the stick and talked me through everything. On ride number one he had me slow the bird and then move the stick from side to side. I met adverse yaw for the first time. All versions of the F-100 acted like they had invented adverse yaw. The F-100A was the worst because it had the smallest tail. The newer models were a bit better; however, all of them could bite you in the butt in a hurry. In a swept wing aircraft at high angles of attack, a movement of the aileron down causes more drag on that side than the up aileron does. This causes the nose to yaw the opposite direction from the roll. The F-100's were especially bad due to their shape and the size of the vertical stabilizer. If you kept your feet on the floor and put the stick right, the bird would roll right, but the nose would yaw left. At higher angles it became worse and, if you really yanked on the pole and slammed the aileron hard over, the bird would roll one way and then snap over the high wing and spin. This is really not a good thing, especially in the traffic pattern. The answer was to coordinate the rudder pedals with the stick to keep the nose pointed where you wanted it to be. In fact you really led with the rudder and followed with the stick. At very high angles, you worked very hard to keep the stick centered and rolled the bird with your feet and controlled the rate of turn with the elevator. My time in the T-28 really paid off, especially the miserable time spent with Earnst running the rudder trim off while I held the T-28 just above a stall. The F-100 was the only aircraft I ever flew that you literally flew with your feet. In fact when I got into really flying the aircraft to its maximum, I learned to add a bit of TOP aileron to tighten the turn. It had very strange flight characteristics. If you learned all of the Hun's bad habits you could really fly it. If you didn't, the loss rate went way up. Philco had the cajones to start me out right on ride one. We were the first class through pilot training after the T-37 replaced the T-28. Only one base had Tweets (T-37's); so, we only had 3 or 4 guys who had never flown a bird that absolutely had to be flown with the rudders. They had a much harder time checking out in the F-100 than the T-28 bunch. I soloed after the minimum number of rides in the 'F' and was a Hun driver!

The school was set up for the absolute minimum number flights in a two seaters. The vast majority of our training was in the F-100C with an IP also in a 'C'. I loved single seat flying then and still do. We progressed from Aircraft Handling to Formation flying and were soon flying all four ship flights. The extracurricular training from Titan and Diamond really helped. The combat patrol formations soon were being done at about the maximum altitude the Hun could get. You had to be very swift to keep in position without using afterburner. The guys who used burner and ran short of gas, were ridiculed by both the IP and the other flight members. We were learning discipline the hard way. The secret was to use the vertical instead of the throttle. When Lead turned into a wide spread formation, the inside element needed to climb until they passed over lead and then dive down to be back in position and matched airspeed. The Out side had to dive, gain speed and cut to the inside and then climb back to match speed and be in position. It sounds easy and it is, after you can intuit all of the moves. I came to realize that this was not just a program for the F-100, but was going to be the foundation for everything I would be called to do for the rest of my flying career. Prior to Combat Crew Training, everything was left to the Fighter Squadron to do. That means that the Line Squadrons spent most of their time training new guys and never could develop the edge they should have.

Dell was very pregnant by this time and was sick and tired of dragging all that stomach around all the time. I was busy as a cat in a sand box and was not very helpful to her. She toughed it out and we had all the plans ready for the new child. We would leave two year old Reid with Jack Brewton and his Lady while Dell was in the hospital. The plan was to take Reid to Brewton's, drop him off and take Dell to the hospital. About 0200 on Feb 3, Dell woke me and said "NOW"! I grabbed all the gear, Reid, and her and headed for the car. She said "Right Now"! I went straight to the Luke Hospital. I wagged Reid into the Hospital with Dell and she was rushed to delivery. Men were not allowed there; so, I took Reid to

Brewton's. I got back to the Hospital at 0430 and I was the father of Margaret Ruth Sparks. Dell and I decided that we might change birth control techniques since that had been a squeaker. Reid spent the next few days with the Brewton's and his nights with me until Dell came home from the Hospital.

I called Louisville to tell mother that she was a grandmother again. She told me that she was going to head for Phoenix whether I wanted her to or not. I went to the Squadron to tell them I couldn't fly that day. It was about 0530 when I arrived there and only the Squadron CC was there. Maj. Thomas was a grumpy man with very little sense of humor. I never saw him fly with students, in fact, he seldom flew. I walked into his office, gave him a cigar, told him I was a new father, and that I couldn't fly that day since I had been up all night. He glared at me and told me that his squadron was not about to schedule around pregnant women and to fly as I was ordered. I blew straight up and told him where to put it. I offered to shove my Gold Bars and my Wings up his fundamental orifice and stomped out. I turned right and bumped into Max Pearson, one our old head IP's. He asked what fight I was headed for. I stuck a cigar into his hand and told him I was a new father. He laughed and asked why the anger. I related what Thomas had said. He grabbed me by the arm, walked into the boss's office, told him he was sending me home and to "keep your cheap mouth shut"! I saw Al Logan as I left, handed him the box of cigars to disperse and went home. Thomas never mentioned that incident again. Louis Braun, Ugga Honk, called me in the next day and semi-apologized for his boss. He told me to never hit a senior officer regardless of how big an ass he was and that he would 'Take Care' of me. The case was closed.

All the airlines were on strike for some reason and mother came from Louisville to Phoenix by Greyhound. By the time she got there, I had Dell and Reid home. Reid was sick, Peggy was brand new and not happy with the world and I was as busy as I could be. There was no way I could get any leave. We were in a mess. Kathleen called me from the Bus Station and took over. I have never been so happy to see anyone. Mother was in her glory! She was able to mother Dell, Reid, Peggy, AKA Piglet, and me all at the same time. She stayed awhile and had us in good shape before she went home, again by bus.

We flew almost every day. We also had Academics every day. We started with F-100 systems and flight characteristic and went from there through classes that were germane to what we were flying. We had classes on Tactics that were really academic and Weapons and Fuses that were very technical. The toughest were reserved Special Weapons. Nuclear Weapons were called 'Special Weapons' for some strange and we had to know all about them. All of us had to go through the Goat Rope to get Top Secret Clearances to become 'Bomb Commanders'. I never wanted to Command a Bomb and wasn't too sure what I was supposed to command it to do. Strategic Air Command (SAC) was responsible for every thing we had to do with Nuke's. At the time almost everyone who flew Tactical Fighters had to be in the Nuke delivery business. The first requirement to be a 'Bomb Commander' was to go through a school. By the time we finished, I was convinced that we were going to be given a box of tubes, wires, uranium, explosives and be told to build one. It was ridiculous. We had zero reason to have to memorize every bit and piece in a Nuke bomb. Rules were rules and shortly, or longly, later, we passed the test on the MK-7 and were on our way to becoming Bomb Commanders.

Dell and I were becoming cramped in the trailer with two kids. I asked her to see if she could find someone who might be interested in buying it. Dell met a Tech Sgt and his wife who needed a place. She worked out a deal where they took over the payments and we took their furniture and some cash. It was a deal for both and we did it. We moved from Glendale to Goodyear into a two bedroom place with a swamp cooler. It was only for a bit over three months until we would move and about the same distance from Luke. A special bonus was that we were only a couple blocks From the Goodyear Naval base. They had a good pool that gave Dell a place to take Reid and relax for no money and no problems. We were now out of the trailer business.

Basic Fighter Maneuvers followed Formation and we started to learn the basic tricks to dog fighting. We had Academics and then started to fly one-on-one with the IP's. They would put us in trail and demonstrate a move. We would swap and they would show a counter move. They would move up on a perch, high and at 4 o'clock or 8 o'clock and attack. We would try a move. They'd put us on a perch and show us a counter. It was a slow building block approach that ended with a capability to attack or defend from attack. The interesting part was, and still is, that some people instinctively do the best thing because they can think in three dimensions. A few folk just never can make that mental shift. I seemed to understand the problem very quickly. Al Logan and a few others were just as fast. It seemed as though I knew what to do and only needed to be put in that three dimensional positional to react properly. I was a very happy camper. I found that I had landed where I ought to be and, just maybe, I could be a fighter pilot.

We had a special student start our F-100 class, Capt. Bill Brothers, USMC, AKA Paladin. He came complete with the business card with the Knight. He managed to breeze through the course an about 2 weeks and came back as an IP. He was our Marine Exchange Officer at Luke and was both a great pilot and Instructor. I was fortunate to be able to fly several sorties with Paladin. About the time we were finishing the Basic Fighter Maneuver section Breezeway, Capt. Bob Fizer, who had just completed the Fighter Weapons School at Nellis, sold our Wing DO on the idea that he could set up a facsimile of the Weapons School Air-To-Air program at Luke for the CCT students. Lt.Col. Buzz Buzze bought the idea and we became the 1st class to go through the program. It was a no holds barred, 17 ride, full-up course of instruction that allowed us to really learn how to 'Fight' the Hun, not to fly it, but to put it on like a shirt and use it to really 'Fight' the bird. Paladin was one of the best along with Louis Braun, Thunder Johnson, and a few others. We were extremely fortunate to be able to learn to really fly the Hun to its' absolute limit before we knew it was dangerous.

The all F-100 models had a problem with Compressor Stalls. A compressor stall occurred normally when the afterburner was lit at high angles of attack. The sudden demand for more air into the engine would cause stagnation in the compressor section of the engine which caused them to stall. The bird would groan, the power would slacken, and there would be this incredible BANG from the aft section. It sounded as though the engine had exploded and would flat get your attention. If you didn't let the nose down it would stall again and again. The noise scared you so bad it was an instinct to slam the stick forward. We quickly learned to relax 'G' for a second prior to jamming the throttle outboard for 'burner. The first time I saw another F-100 compressor stall was spectacular. I'd had several of them; everyone had them often; however, to see fire shoot out of an aircraft was something else! The F-100C with the older P-19 engine had more than their share of compressor stalls. Learning to use the bird required learning to keep the stalls to a minimum. You only learn by creating automatic responses to things and reacting properly. I was learning the wear the Hun like a shirt.

I did rather well early on and managed to score a few victories on Iceman. I was starting to believe that my excrement had the odor of roses. That is a very bad thing for a student; so, I flew my first ride with Ugga Honk. Louie was not your standard svelte fighter pilot. He was called 12 'G' Ugga Honk because he could pull more 'G' than anyone. He wore a very old 'G' suit that had holes in all the bladders, loose strings, and a rip in the attachment hose. He would put students on his wing and start a turn that became tighter and tighter until you were looking down a 22 barrel about to blackout and he'd crane his neck and say "Fuel Check, Honks". If you were lucky, you could look down only with your eyes, check your fuel gauge and squeak an answer. He'd then tighten up the turn and put you away. We briefed and we flew. I was beaten like a rug on every engagement. He rode me and kicked my butt until my nose bled. When we were riding back in the bread wagon, he said "Don't feel bad Sparky, sometime you're even hard to track". I could have sat on a cigarette paper and swung my feet. After a very thorough debriefing, he took me to the bar and bought me a Martini. He grinned and asked who he should fly with the next day and I told him Al Logan. The next evening Al was at the bar with Louie looking like something the dog dragged in and Louie asked him the same question and al told him, Roger Parish. Roger was about our best Pilot and had soloed when he was 14. The next night he looked like Al and me and we all help Ugga Honk pick his next victim. That course was the best thing for my development as a fighter pilot ever. I became a pretty damned good pilot before I made 1st Lt. If you challenge folk, give them good instruction, and then really work them, they will be a whole bag better than if you coddle them, protect them from harm and make sure that Safety Is Always First.

We went from single ship fights to two versus two and finally, four versus four. The Class made it through the whole program without scratching an airplane. We also became very confident in flying the F-100 regardless of its' strange flight characteristics. The more we pushed the envelope, we became more and more able to wear the bird like a shirt and not ever think of flying, but to put it where ought to be because that would be best. It has been a long time since I was a student at Luke. I was stationed at Nellis 3 times after I was a student and graduated from the Fighter Weapons School as Top Gun; however, the 6 months at Luke in '59 taught me all the basic things I ever needed. The rest were wonderful, but the basics were courtesy of Honk and his crowd.

We went from Air-to-Air to Air-to-Mud. It would seem that gunnery would be easier than Air-to-Air; however, dirt has a probability of kill of almost 100%. In Air-to-Air you are high enough to recover after a screw-up before you hit the deck. If you screw up in the gunnery pattern, the dirt is very close and very likely to end everything suddenly. We started to go to the Gila Bend Ranges every day. Low angle gunnery, Strafing and skip bombing were first, followed by rocket firing and 30 degree dive bombing. 45 degree work was next. We slowly master the art of maneuvering to be at the proper dive angle, lining up the target, getting the right airspeed, and having the pipper (sight) pass through the target at the right altitude. We learned how to correct for wind and how to salvage a bad set-up in order to hit the target. It took a lot of tries at hurling your body at the ground before you got it right. We always had an IP in the scoring tower for every mission. That is not exactly the best job in the world since it is hot in south Arizona, noisy on the range, and you sure as hell aren't flying. I remember starting to get a bit cocky and was back to odorless excrement when Louie gave me another lesson. I was really pressing the foul line on the strafe panels to win a bet with Al Logan and Roger. I made two passes and was going to press in and fire out on the last pass. As I pulled out Honk said "Son, if I have to look down at you one more time, you are toast!" He added 100 hundred boners to my name as well. A boner cost a nickel to the beer fund. He also fouled me off the strafe target and I got a zero for the ride. We were betting a nickel a hole in the target and I was making about $300 per month. The ride cost me about 10 bucks.

Our last course was in Aerial Gunnery. We only fired at the banner at Luke. A banner is about 20' long and 5' tall that is trailed behind a tow ship on a 1200' cable. The T-33 would tow it at about 300 knots and, I think, 20,000' altitude. The idea was to start out above the banner with it at your ten or two and make a maneuver so you were passing through about 1500 feet from the banner at about a 15 degree angle when you fired at it. Now this sound like it would be easy. It was tough! I was close to tops in my class and I averaged about 8% on that damned thing. My high score was 15% and I missed it all together twice. Even Honk had problems getting high scores. We had over half the class that only hit it once or twice in the whole course. Everyone was glad to be going to Nellis where we could shoot at the Dart, a towed target made with triangular horizontal and vertical surfaces in an X shape that was towed by another F-100 and could be maneuvered in three dimensions. It was now late May and time to leave Luke. A good thing happened at about this time, all of us from Pilot training completed our require 18 months and were promoted to Silver Bars. The pay raise to 1Lt. was nice as was the change from Butter Bars to Silver ones. Butter bars are by definition very stupid and in need of much supervision.

Dell and I had both enjoyed Luke and the Valley Of The Sun. We would have stayed there happily, but we needed to finish the Combat Crew Training and then go to our first Squadron assignment. After the Air-To-Ground was completed, all of our scores and assessments were totaled and we were given a list of assignments available to our class. We were allowed to pick our by class standing. Roger finished first and took Bitburg, the only German base. Jack Brewton was next and took George AFB and F-104's. I was next and took Itazuke Japan since all the European bases available were in France. France was about as unfriendly as it was possible to be in the late 50's. All of the Stateside TAC units spent at least half their time on Temporary Duty, TDY. Dell and I needed to have some time together before I started into the long TDY's and decided to try for an oversea assignment for our first tour. Jack Jacoby; a classmate started bugging me about Itazuke. He wanted that assignment a ton and worked on me big time to swap him for Etain, France. His wife even bugged Dell. I talked to Dell about the swap and found that she was not all that shot with going to Japan with two children. There were rumors that we would be pulling our fighter units out of the French bases soon; so, I called Jack and we went down to Personnel and swapped. Less than a week later the 388th at Etain was re-designated as the 49th and given orders to move to Spangdahlem Germany. My orders were changed to reflect that move. Spangdahlem was only 16 Kilometers from Bitburg where I had wanted to go all along. I lucked out once more!

We planned the move to 'Vegas to allow Al Logan and I would to go in my car, sign in, get places to live, and head for Survival School at Stead AFB. Dell, Betty, and our children would come up in his Chevy with Air Conditioning. Al and I left about midnight to stay out of the heat and drove on some of the crappiest roads outside West Virginia. We rolled into the Las Vegas Valley just after sunrise and were first in line to sign in at Nellis. We drove down the Salt Lake Highway toward North Las Vegas and stopped at the Vandemeer Apartments where several of us had selected to live. Al and I rented two, two-bedroom places that were next door to each other. I unloaded the trailer with the Lambretta on it, bought a six-pack, and we were ready to head for Reno. The Ladies arrived as planned the day before we got back from starving school.

CHAPTER FOUR
COMBAT CREW TRAINING - NELLIS

Al and I got back to the Vandemeer Apartments the day after Betty and Dell arrived with our families. Both places were furnished, shabbily but furnished; so, there wasn't much moving in since what furniture we had was in storage until we left Nellis. They both looked wonderful. Betty was quite pregnant with their second and needed Al back. Both of our ladies told us we looked like Death Eating Crackers. I weighed 150 lbs when I was married, weighed the same when I went to Lackland and had worked up to 175 after almost 2 years in the USAF and was in great shape. I came back from Starving School at 158. Al had also lost 17 pounds in the two weeks. We both were in great shape when we went into the woods. Our F-86 Captain lost 28 pounds during our sojourn in the North.

Academics for the Combat Crew started the Monday after we came back. We had a whole weekend off. Nellis was a continuation of what had started at Luke. The first thing was an introduction to the F-100D. The D was a single seat F and unlike the C, had flaps. There were a bag of different versions of the 'D'. The training for each variant was left to units that owned them or we would have been at Nellis forever. My Squadron Commander was Major Hoot Gibson who was a Korean Ace. He was an extremely good pilot, very friendly, outgoing, and cared for the students like a Grandfather. We were lucky again. The Instructors were all experienced Fighter Pilots who also were there to teach. I met my Instructor, Captain Lloyd Boothby, on the first day in the squadron and we remained friends until his death in '07. Lloyd, AKA Mouthby, was the funniest man I have ever known. He knew every joke in the world, was a raconteur of the highest caliber, and was the best Instructor I ever flew with. Boots was not the best pilot by any stretch, but he could explain things better than anyone else. He told Al and me that he ALWAYS had the top gun in every class. We didn't let him down. We were 1 and 2.

We started with some Air-To-Air to get back in the swing of things and added the AIM-9 Sidewinder to our bag of tricks. The AIM-9 had a heat seeker head that homed in on the hottest thing it could see and left a slight zigzag track, thus, Sidewinder. It could only be carried on the inboard station of the Hun. The rack consisted of a whole new pylon, Type-9, for the inboard that was much bigger than the standard pylon and extended lower as well. With two of the things, you had about as much area as the vertical stabilizer. If you got the bird into much of a yaw, it would snap with about no warning. The tendency of all F-100's to have adverse yaw made it a most interesting addition to the bird. We started out by carrying a single Sidewinder and learning how to understand the meaning of the Rattlesnake chirp it made when it saw something hot. We would drop back on the IP and center him in the reticule of the sight and move up, down, right, and left to see where the center of the seeker was located. If we carried more than one, we would check each one for alignment and remember each missile. We learned to keep away from the sun, what the moon looked like to the seeker and became knowledgeable of the only working missile in the inventory. We were allowed to shoot a live missile at a 5" HAVAR Rocket. The IP carried 4 of them and would put us into an off set trail, fire a HAVAR, BREAK HARD away from our position and clear us to fire. We could then arm the missile, center the HAVAR in the sight, get a tone, and fire. It was a real kick to watch the Sidewinder come off the rail and leave its signature track and hit the HAVAR. The first day Al was first to shoot. When the 'Winder' cleared the rail it went into a huge loop, came down at our six and blew up below us. That's not exactly what we were expecting. The rest went as advertised and Al got to re-fly the mission. After we were familiar with the AIM-9, we went into a series of missions to learn how to use the missile under real conditions. That's when we found that the bird really did not like to be at high angles of attack with a TYPE-9 on board. Everyone in the class departed the bird in the next few days; however, because we had been taught so well at Luke, everyone unloaded, caught to sideslip, and regained control. I snapped three times in one 25 minute fight. We had a Squadron of F-100's from one of the stateside bases come to Nellis for AIM-9 training during this time. They lost 3 aircraft after the first week and the Fit Hit The SHAN. I had just landed from a flight with Lonnie Ferguson when everyone was grounded until a briefing was given about the F-100 flight characteristics. Lonnie closed the door, asked who had snapped the bird that day, got the real answer, gave us a GOOD story about how we never flew at high 'G' with a TYPE-9, smiled and left. We kept up our training while the REAL Fighter Pilots flew under unrealistic rules.

I met John Boyd about that time since he came over to our CCTS Class to brief his "30 second Boyd" maneuver. John Boyd and Cal Davey were instructors in the Fighter Weapons School at the time and were trying to figure out how to show people a method of comparing unlike aircraft to develop the best Tactics to use against the other Aircraft. John had come up with a move that, according to him, would flush anyone out from behind him and allow him to get a shot in 30 seconds. If that sounds like a free lunch, it was. We had already been taught it as a last ditch defensive move by Breezeway at Luke. It was to be used when someone had you saddled and was about to shoot. You would steepen your bank and keep increasing your 'G' until you were about to stall, then pull full back on the stick in order to generate as much angle of attack as possible. You would grab the stick with both hands to keep the ailerons from moving and jam full top rudder. The bird would stand on its tail, shudder like mad, do a near flat plate pivot, and lose about 200 knots. If you didn't have enough smash to go over the top, you could do the same thing except use bottom rudder and lose about 100 knots. If the attacker had his stuff anywhere near a sack, he would go for altitude and be ready to come down on you and eat your lunch because you were out of airspeed. They were spectacular to watch, but were really not of much use except against another F-100 or something similar. An F-86 would just kill you. I got to fly with John and I would bet a ton Louie would gobble him up.

I went to the Bar with Boots for Beer Call and Cal Davy and John Boyd were both there holding forth on Energy Maneuverability, whatever the hell that was. Cal had a great big plastic egg with him in the bar and was drawing maneuvers on it by having one arrow do something and then have the other arrow do an out of plane counter to show why vertical maneuvers whip flatter maneuvers. It was the first time I had seen 'Cal Davy's Egg' and it was a wonderful teaching aid. Both Cal and John were in the bag and Al and I wound up becoming their star pupils for the nonce. Boots was roaring with laughter and Al and I were backing up with both of the Weapons School IP's yammering away.

Boyd had a habit of getting right in your face and shouting to make a point. He managed to get spit on everyone in five feet. Cal was almost as bad. By the time we escaped, we were both wet with Energy Maneuverability spit!

Betty was very tired of being pregnant and Al agreed with her. This was before the USAF discovered that wives and dependents needed to have someone check on them occasionally. We were both scheduled to fly the day her water broke and Al took her to the Nellis Hospital. Males, other than Doctors, were not allowed anywhere near the delivery ward, so Al went to the Squadron and was told to suit up and fly. I landed about 15 minutes before Al did and asked Boots if I could skip debriefing and headed for the hospital. Only 'Family' could visit the new Mothers. Dell had gotten there earlier and informed them that she was Betty's sister. I walked in a responded to 'WHO?' with, "I'm the father". I knew enough not to tell the truth about newborn looks and did appropriate noises about Erick. A nurse came in and said that she had the maddest Lt she had ever seen demanding to see Betty. Betty asked who it was and was told that the guy said he was the husband! Betty's exact words were, "Let him in, I want him to meet the Father!" Erick still calls me 'DAD'.

CHAPTER FIVE
COMBAT CREW TRAINING - STEAD

Al Logan and I had arranged to ride up to Stead AFB with Harvey Houzenga (pronounced Hows-en-gay), a 6' 3", 195pound, ex Navigator who had been a classmate of mine in pilot training at Malden. Harvey was a much laid back, great sense of humor, friendly guy who could eat more than anyone I ever met and stay fit. Harvey had a great set of wheels; bachelors could afford a Thunderbird with all the bells and whistles. We left Las Vegas and drove US-95 to Sparks Nevada and ate a huge meal to prepare for the Survival School. It consisted of two parts, Survival and preparation for POW status. The survival part was done in the Sierras over a large area of what was then wilderness. The Prisoner of War Camp was on Stead proper, isolated from the main base. We went through a bunch of classes first. Some were good and some not very swift. All of the POW resistance classes were first class. Most of the Survival classes were standard filler at best. We could go into Sparks or Reno for at night during the first week but were restricted to the base after that. Al Logan and I had spent a bunch of time outdoors as kids. Al was from Tishomingo Oklahoma, where his father had been a cowboy all his life. Real rope and horse type cow puncher. Albert Lee was an only child, born in the depression, and the first member of his family to go to college. Al had been a Bull Rider, Saddle-Bronc Rider, Roper, and a Welterweight Golden Gloves Boxer through High School and Oklahoma State with the nose to prove it. The flattened nose was really a gift from a Brahma Bull but boxing sounded better. Al and I had become the best of friends and could manage to get into trouble while putting money in the collection plate. Harvey was a great big pussy cat by comparison.

I don't know anyone, other one guy from New York City, who went through the Academic classes on 'Woods Wandering' who thought it was worth anything. After the classes we were separated into groups of 6 for the 5 day, 47 mile survival trek. Charley Summers, Dave Pine, Albert Lee, me, Harvey, and an F-86 Captain headed for Japan who had to go through 'Starve and Suffer' on the way, were together for the week. We boarded trucks that took us into the High Sierra above the Squaw Valley area. In '59 nothing was there but trees. We were handed over to our Instructor, a young Airman 2nd who lacked confidence and seemed to be at a loss for everything. Our Instructor, 'Faithful Indian Guide' didn't even seem to know where east was at sunrise. The kid was a city boy and was really out of his depth. We were issued some parachute cloth, a ratty sleeping bag, a parachute harness, quite a bit of parachute cord, a compass, a map each, a carbine bayonet, a shelter half, and very few items from the seat kit survival pack. Each squad was given some beef to make jerky, a hatchet, and a live rabbit. Faithful Indian Guide had a 100 pound pack with all sorts of goodies including bacon, real eggs, and coffee for his sole use. We were given instructions on where we were to go and a general area in which to spend each of the 5 nights we were in the field. We made packs from the harness, cord, and parachute material. We had our obligatory meeting to figure out who was to do what and to whom. Our Captain would be the boss, Al and I would be the guides, Harvey would try and do all the navigating, Dave Pine would carry the rabbit. Summers was the all purpose infielder. We found a yellow brick road and headed for Oz.

During the trek we had a two pemmican bars a day, ate the rabbit, made jerky to eat, scrounged for food in the high mountains where there is damned little to eat and ended up moving 47 miles on something like 300 calories a day in 5 days. This area was used for training by all summer classes and had hardly any wildlife because it had been scared off. We were in a Wilderness Area and could not just rip up a Beaver Pond and grab the fish. Fishing lures were forbidden and fire arms were verboten. The only things I caught the whole week were 6 mussels, 4 minnows, and a snake. We ate them in about 4 bites each. The whole thing was poor joke. I figured out that if you slept on the ground that you would be sore and tired. If you walked long distances up and down tall hills with little to eat you would be hungry. If you are above 10'000 feet at night with a very shabby sleeping bag you will be extremely cold, and last but not least, if some young idiot goes up wind and fries eggs and makes coffee you will be tempted to kill and eat him.

The 3rd day out our fearless leader called in our Indian Guide, introduced him to Harvey and promised that if we got even one more sniff of food cooking, Harvey would eat him on the spot. Dave Pine carried the rabbit for 3 days until it was his time to become dinner. Al handed Bugs to me to snap his neck and skin him. Dave thought that we should keep his innards and make soup. Al and I advised him strongly not to do that! Charley agreed with Al and me. Dave decided to cook the guts and see what they would be like. We were sitting around our fire eating Rabbit pieces cooked on sticks when Dave picked up the canteen cup with the gut-soup and tried a bite. There was silence until he made this horrible face and croaked "Eyeball". We roared. Dave decided that if he stripped the intestines they would be nutritious. Nobody else needed that.

The next day Brother Pine was feeling poorly. By noon he was empty from both ends, stank like bad Kimshi, and had trouble walking. By evening he was reeling. The rule was that if you didn't finish the trek, you washed back a class and did it again. Al and I handed Pine's pack to the boss and took turns carrying Dave. For the next two days it was drag Dave, rest, drag Dave, rest. It was two very long days. Our Indian Guide was threatened with death by Harvey if he opened his mouth. We all made the 47 miles and Dave was able to walk the last few miles. We had gotten a bit grumpy by the last day. Al and I managed to get into an argument about the size of a squirrel. We were both quite hot about it until Harvey started to laugh at us. I think we might have been tired.

The last night was a Border Crossing exercise. All the Indian Guides and their supervisors were pulled out to set up a moving barrier of people. Our job was to evade them and make it to the rendezvous point undetected. This was to be done in pairs. Logan and Sparks paired up and set off for a good place to hide and check the area. We put Dave Pine and Harvey together since Harvey was the strongest. Charley and our F-86 driver were paired. Al and I really boogied up a steep slope and onto a shelf. That gave us a good look at the roads and trails we had to cross before dark. We decided that the canyon that started directly below us was far too steep for any of the Cadre to patrol. If we could make it down that canyon without busting a leg, we'd be way ahead of the game. We headed down just before twilight with the sun at our back. It was a real bitch but, no Cadre was there, and we were ahead of everyone. We followed a small stream, keeping to the willows, until we came to the last area of real concern, a logging road. We crept up to the road and waited until we could see movement in the moonlight and spotted the guards positions. We slipped around them and waited a good 30 minutes to insure the area was empty. We sprinted across the open area one at a time. Al went first and I was to follow after 10 minutes. As I started to run, a Jeep started around a bend to my left and I dived for cover right into the creek. We both froze, Al to keep quiet and I because the damned water was just above freezing! Al came over to where I was hiding in the water and asked if I was ok. I just said "Ribbit—Ribbit" and he snorted.

We made our way to a small clearing and I got a rubdown. We were only a couple of miles from the official end of the trek, but we didn't trust anyone and detoured way east in the woods and came into the clearing, a campground, by the back way. We sneaked up to a hiding place only 20 feet or so from their bonfire and watched. Shortly a guy came up to report in. They grabbed him and put him in a holding pen and told him he was a Prisoner! Al and I just sat where we were. Al slipped down behind the guards and stole two Oranges and two Donuts and we had a snack. We were hiding straight across the fire from the guards, but they were fire dazzled and never saw us. We even took turns napping until 1 minute before the end of the exercise and walked up to the food, took an orange and said HI! The guards jumped and we got on the truck to take us back to Stead.

We started the three day Prisoner Of War exercise the next day. We had finished all the POW classes before went for the walk in the woods. The POW related classes all made sense and were worth the whole two weeks. The primary Instructor had been a POW in Korea and did not speak with forked tongue. He had worked for several years to be able to pass this vital information to us. This definitely was not your standard USAF Bull Crap. It was taken very seriously.

We entered the Camp on schedule and it was indeed a Bear! A huge USAF Master Sergeant with flaming red hair was the Camp Commandant. Everyone on the Camp Cadre was in Russian style uniforms with Red Stars on their shoulder boards and hats. They all looked and sounded mean. Most were also very good at their jobs with only a few should have not been there. It is extremely hard to find people who could do the kind of work required for that job.

We were 'housed' in dirt bunkers with zero sanitation devices. Pseudo beatings were happening and humiliation was rife. Screaming was gentle abuse and we were roughed up a lot more than I ever would have thought possible. Everyone was bounced off walls and slapped on the body. Sleep was a joke for the total time we were in jail. We were kept moving or were tied so we couldn't move at all. We had just come from a week of being very hungry, we had used up just about all our reserves, and we were now being pushed to our limit. A very interesting thing happened to me while I was being interrogated by the real expert. I had just come from being tossed about and body slammed a few times before he came in and started asking for the information we had been given to hide. There was a phrase used to stop the exercise as it was at that point and ask questions or clarify something. The phrase was 'Academic Situation'. I was busting my butt to not answer anything and doing fairly well when the interrogator called for an Academic Situation. He told me that I was doing what was proper, but to talk to him and see what happened in order for me to learn a lesson. I found that talking was a disaster! It was far worse than a discourse with a Jesuit. He had me by the short hairs in a hurry! That scared me a ton and alone it was worth the cost of admission! He stopped the interrogation session when I finally totally clammed up and called in the misanthropes. They banged me around a while and put me in the locker. It was one of a row of standard wooden wall lockers. They put wooden pallets in the bottom until it would be extremely crowded for my 3 year old and then stuffed me in. I was in a position with my knees up against my chin, bent over until it was very hard to breathe, my body jammed up against the sides of the locker. That was true misery. There was a hood over my head, my time sense was shot, and I just could not believe this was happening to me. I have never been so uncomfortable. I couldn't scratch my nose. It rapidly went from discomfort to pain. It seemed as though I was in that thing a week. I would hear somebody wail and then, Blam! They'd hit his box with a club. I managed to keep quiet, was hit anyway. I was luck that I was empty because it scared me crosswise. I decided that I would keep quiet until they opened the door and then whap the guard in the chops! I was really looking forward to smacking the guy. After what seemed an eternity, the door jerked open, I took a mighty swing at the guard, missed, and fell on my face. I couldn't move anything for a while. He calmly grabbed me by the back of my flight suit, dragged me out the door, and kicked my butt.

I was put on KP duty in the prison yard and given some slop to make into soup. I was trying to break some wood up into kindling to cook the goop in a garbage can we were issued when the Guard, who had taught us hand to gland fighting, kicked me in the gut. I doubled up and fell sideways. I muttered something about the number of breast on his mother and rolled over. He grabbed me by the shirt, twisted it to choke me, and jerked me to my feet. He stuck his face in mine, laughed and spit on me. I yelled "Academic Situation". He pushed me back, laughed, and spit on me again. I had a fair sized stick of fire wood in my hand and I got him right across side of his neck. He tried to grab me and I got him in the face and dropped him. I was going to put him away when one of my classmates grabbed me. I was frog-marched to the Camp Commandant who started into a tirade. I demanded an Academic Situation. He grabbed me by my throat to shake me. I still had my stick and I whapped him in the arm as hard as I could. He fell over backward still holding me off him by the throat, hollering "Academic Situation". I kept trying to break anything I could until we hit the floor. He said. "Are you through?" I calmed down a bit and asked him if his goons were through spitting on me. He started to tell me I was in a POW camp and I told him I was In Nevada, could damned near see Reno and that No One could spit on me and live. I added that he was an enlisted man, his guard was an enlisted man and that I was an Officer. I told him we could keep up this crap or we could go before a Courts Martial. He let me go and told me that I would be a dead person if this were real. I told him his idiot guard would also have been dead had this had been real. He said that I might have a point. We had a short discussion and I was taken out and made to dig a hole in the ground. I was shot with blanks, then put in the grave and covered up.

I was sent back to my job of building fires. I looked over and saw Al Logan talking to several of our guys while they were looking in at us. Knowing Al, I figured that they were up to something. The same guard I had hit with the stick limped over and started to bitch about what we were doing. Al kicked down a barrier and led a charge of about 20 guys. He jumped into the air and kicked the guard in the gut with both feet and knocked him into the fire. They grabbed the garbage can we had been heating and poured it on him. He left a lot worse for wear. Albert Lee then dug a hole, was shot, covered up, and joined me in stirring more garbage. Neither Al nor I were hassled the rest of the day. The exercise was over at dark that day.

We had a day of debriefings that were outstanding. I had a solo session with the big Master Sergeant that was very enlightening. We agreed that I would probably be killed if I were ever a POW. Leo Thorsness told me in '73 that they wouldn't let you die since that would be too easy on you. The Survival Trek taught hardly any of us anything and was a waste of time. It did make us tired enough for the Camp to be very real. The POW Camp was priceless. In anything like that some of the staff will get carried away. It must be a tremendous temptation to give Officers a ration. I should never have hit that guard. He sure as hell should have never spit on me. He had been around long enough that he should have known I would react. He would have been in the hospital a long time if he had spit on Logan. We were released to the joys of Reno with food chits, a roll of nickels, some chips, and a desire to have several jars of brown whiskey. The next day we rode back to Las Vegas with Harvey.

CHAPTER SIX
FERRY FLIGHT – FEBRUARY 1962

Tones Babes and I had been at Nellis for the F-105 RTU that lasted 90+ days and all of the money we could steal. It was the worst course I have ever seen. Jim Beam, of Seymour Johnson fame, was the Squadron Commander and was in a fight with Maintenance the whole time I was there. There were about 75 Thuds at Nellis and we seldom had more that 10 flyable at anytime. Jim Bean was several bricks short of a load to start with; therefore, made up for his lack of brightness by being surly and obnoxious to boot. Wilbur Grumbles, 49TFW CC had been in the first class and had managed to cause urination among the Nellis MFWICs by telling them that they ran a very shabby school. Since Lt. Col. Bean couldn't get to Wilbur J., he got to the troops that followed him, namely us. The course finally came to a sloppy finish and we left with less than 30 hours each from a 75-hour syllabus. One of the worst things about the course was that there was zero instruction in instrument procedures at any time. There was a simulator that was broken for the whole time and we all left without any instrument instruction or practice. The F-105 was the first USAF Fighter with Vertical Tapes instead of round gauges and had an entirely different navigation presentation. That didn't bother Jim Bean since he only flew in the desert and never at night. All of us were happy to be gone from that happy camp whether we could fly weather or not.

We went to mobile Alabama in February just in time to happen upon the coldest weather on record. Mobile Bay froze over for the first time in history the day I got there. They immediately sent me to Long Island to pick up a new Thud from Republic. That is when I realized that I probably needed to figure out how to fly the big bitch in the goo. I gave myself instruction on the way to Mobile from Farmingdale and managed to land in a 400' ceiling and about 1 mile visibility. I was not a happy camper. Ralph Schneider, Tony Gangol, and 2 or 3 other guys were also not cheering about our skill levels. We met with a very sharp Major from the Ferry Group and explained our problem. He suggested that we set up our own instrument school and gave us 2 birds twice a day to fly for about a week. We taught ourselves the tricks of the Vertical Tapes and new Horizontal Situation Indicator (H.S.I) and also built up about another 10 hours of thud time. We waited for good ferry weather and enough aircraft to fly to Spangdahlem only to discover that all of the KB-50s were grounded due to frequent explosions.

We were sent to Seymour Johnson to fly home via

Newfoundland and the Azores without tankers. When we arrived at See My Johnson, we were told that the DuckButts, C-54 "Rescue" aircraft were not available since they were busy recovering the Chimpanzee, Ham. We were charmed as usual. We sat around S.J. for a decision and were launched at 0-Dark Thirty without tankers or DuckButts to fly to Earnest Harmon AB Newfoundland, 30 minutes on the ground, and then to Lajes, Azores. From Lajes, it was less than 1000 miles to Spangdahlem. We were first off with another flight an hour later led by Danny Salmon. Cecil Juanarena was our leader and Tones Babes was #3 with me on his wing. We joined up in the pitch black and went into the weather and stayed in the goo for three hours. Cecil January was normally a good pilot; BUT that night he absolutely screwed the pooch to a fair-thee-well. He kept his lights on bright flash for the entire flight (blinds the wingmen) and claimed to have radio and Navigation Aid problems.

Tones Babes had to lead from his number three position since January never relinquished the lead. I figured that we were in deep doodoo when we missed Boston about 60 miles out to sea. January kept the lead and we never hit any checkpoint all the way to Newfoundland. We finally got out of the weather about dawn when we were over the Gulf Of Saint Lawrence and were able to look down at all of that ice until we made it to Earnest Harmon about 20 minutes later. Fearless Leader recovered his gauges and radio and then decided to do an Air Show for the SAC pukes. We made a Diamond Pass down the ramp that also laid a solid layer of Ice Fog right over the runway since it was minus 50 degrees. We then had to land using the ILS and had under ½ mile vis. By now all three wingman were ready to cut January's throat and/or roast him over a slow fire.

We taxied in on glare ice and parked in the refueling pits for gas and a VERY quick turn. We walked into the Ops Building and were given a quick briefing on the next leg to Lajes, 1480 nautical miles away. It was a bit of. " Go That-Away". Fearless Lead was still determined to keep the lead and we manned the birds and started them. The requirement for the quick turn was the extreme low temperature. If the Birds Cold Soaked with the systems not operating for an hour, they would start to leak and we would not be able to fly. There were NO Hangers and we would have stuck for several days. Shortly after we started, Lead had a Maintenance Man stick his head in the Hell Hole door and I thought that we were stuck. Cecil's Radio came on loud and clear and he said " Shut 'em down, I'll be ready in about an hour". Tones asked what he said and I told him " He said that he would meet us in the Azores". We taxied out and left Lead. The flight to the Azores was a piece of cake. Tony was smooth as silk and put the bird on NAV HOLD and let it cruise-climb. That really means that we flew a great circle route and used the most efficient fuel procedures that we had. We arrive with about 1500 pounds more gas that planned and almost 20 minutes ahead of schedule. We landed, refueled, and filed out for Spangdahlem. We got airborn in under an hour and had another textbook flight home. Cecil got home the next day with Danny Salmon and was a bit pissed that we had left him. We decided that all of us had heard exactly the same thing from Juanarena, SEE YOU IN THE AZORES! We still stick to the story regardless of what January   says.

CHAPTER SEVEN
CHARLIE FOXTROT FLIGHT

Paul Craw came to Takhli about month after the 563TFS arrived from McConnell in '65. He was among our first replacements. The 'D' Flight Commander, Bob Wistrand, had been killed in Laos and Paul was to be his replacement. Wisty had been in ADC and then became a Golden Arm and flew acceptance test in Taiwan for about 3 years. He had quite a bit of F-105 time; however, he had zero TAC time and knew zip about our formation, Tactics, and all of the other things required to lead a Flight in a Combat Squadron. The assistant Flight CC was a guy from F-100's in England with over 2500 hours of TAC time who, unfortunately had a very wide yellow streak up his backbone and was about as useful as tits on a boar. He only had about 100 hours in the Thud and was not even a flight lead. I had been leading 'D' flight since we arrived. Paul and Marty Case, an experienced F-100 driver, arrived together and Paul asked me to check them both out. I led Paul for four flights before he thought he had enough checkout time and he made me an offer I couldn't refuse. He wanted to lead the "Best Bunch Of Chicken Fuckers

77

In The World", He told me that I could sit around and try and scrounge up a Flight of four to lead (FAT LUCK), OR, I could be Chicken Fucker Three. I had a couple of beers and decided that I would rather fly with Paul than sit on my ass and hope for a flight since I was in the bottom half of the Squadron rank structure. Kile Berg had been flying my #2 since we arrived and we had known each other for 3 years at Spangdahlem. Paul decided that He would lead, Kile would fly his wing, I would be #3 and Marty Case would fly #4. We then proceeded to fly 39 consecutive Combat sorties in that order with no changes. Basically, Paul had formed "The Best Bunch of Chicken Fuckers He Could Find".

The best thing about Charlie Foxtrot Flight was that we really liked each other. We rapidly came to also totally trust each other as well. Briefings were incredibly easy since we knew what each guy could do and what to expect from each CF. Typical briefing went something like, "Same old crap, let's look at the Photos and see what we can do with this piece of shit". We would spend 30 to 45 minutes looking at the photos and talking to each other until Paul would say "That's enough", and that was that. We really worked on being very accurate with our ordnance and, if we missed, got really ragged by everyone in the flight and had to buy booze. We got so we could home the MER Rack on 'pairs' and only drop two bombs on a single pass. We seldom needed to make more than one pass to whack a target. This left us with 4 bombs on the centerline, whatever was on the outboards, and the gun to RECCE. It was a real kick to be a CF.

Paul Craw was a bit over six-foot, calm, almost scary direct stare, and complete confidence. Kile Berg was about 5'10", looked a bit like Denis the Menace, had a swagger in his walk, and always looked like he was about to sass someone. I was 6' weighed about 195, acted like a typical obnoxious Fighter Pilot, and tried to seem fearless. Marty Case was about 5' 11", quiet, listened intensely, had a very strong aura of competence, and, like all of us, was completely loyal. I have never been able to fly with any group that quite like the Charlie Foxtrots. Our poop had an intense odor of flowers and stank not a bit. We really were sure that we were the original 'Meanest S.O.B. in The Valley'.

CHAPTER EIGHT
EB-66 AND F-105 RADAR KILLS IN 1965

The first EB-66 Squadron arrived at Takhli in mid May, I think, after the 563rd had been there since 18 April. We didn't have the foggiest what they did for a living and what an EWO was. One of the best EB-66 drivers was a guy named Rube Autrey. Rube graduated from the USAF with two or three stars and was a super troop. Paul Craw had been at Tahkli for a couple of weeks and was kicking his flight, The Charlie Chicken F***** (Charlie Foxtrots), into shape. We normally saving our out-board ordnance for road RECCE after we hit nearly any assigned target. Rube and Paul were hoisting a few brown brews and learning what each of us did for a living. Rube was unhappy because he could find any Radar in SEA; however, he couldn't kill anything since he had zero ordnance. Paul was unhappy because he couldn't find any Radars to kill with all of the stuff we carried.

After a few brown brews Rube and Charlie Foxtrot decided that Rube would find them and we would kill them. That is a very simple solution of the

Radar Detection problem. A few days after the Radar search idea was born, Rube and The Charlie Foxtrots were scheduled to fly at the same time. Paul and Rube arranged to rendezvous at a spot somewhere near Vihn after we had hit our assigned target. We all had Rockets and a full gun remaining for the RECCE. We joined up with Rube and he led with us in trail at about 3,000 back. He dropped down to about 1000' and told us that he thought he had a target right on his nose and would pass directly over it, holler, and break up and left. He dropped down to under 500 and we followed at about 3000 back. He said that it would be a 'Yaggi' array, whatever the hell that is. About 15 miles further he yelled that 'it' was under him and broke up and left. We didn't see squat and pulled up into a circle over the spot. One of his EWO's came up and said, "Look for a bed spring hanging in a tree"! Someone said, " I've got it!" and rolled in for a gun pass. I followed and saw what looked like a bedspring on a rack and whapped it with a pod of 2.75 Rockets. We hit every thing we could see in the area and Rube's folk seemed to be very happy.

We finished our RECCE and flew home and debriefed with Rube who was very happy. We managed to join-up with Rube a few more times with a success rate of better that one Radar Site for every two tries. Our best day was maybe 3 weeks later when Rube found us a Real Live Radar Dome on the coast between Vinh and Than Hoa that was looking toward Yankee Station. I do not know what was under the dome except that it was Radar and was operating.

There were also two Height Finders along with the domed Radar aimed at Yankee Station. The Radars all were operating and the Height Finders were nodding away when we made our first pass. I think we had 2 M-117, GP bombs and two each Rocket pods outboard. We smacked the Dome with Bombs and then nailed the Height Finders with the gun. The Dome and its Radar were small pieces and we blew both Height Finders into the Gulf Of Tonkin. We also managed to whack some obstreperous guns that were around the site along with some barracks. Rube and his folk were VERY Happy. We debriefed INTEL, Bad Move, and went about our way. 2nd AIRDIV became very irate and decided that the next guy who did anything like that would have his pecker severely smacked. It became a rule that you couldn't hit anything not pre-approved by McNamara. We were ordered not to ever join up with a B-66 and smack Radars. At that time, Rube and his friends knew where every SAM Site in the North was and what its state of readiness was. That was about six weeks before the first missile lifted off from the Hanoi area on July 24, so much for USAF leadership.

I contacted Paul Craw and Marty Case, Charlie Foxtrot Lead and #4, and asked them to look at this thing. Marty has forwarded the information to Charlie Foxtrot 3, Kyle Berg, for his input. Paul answered that he had no problems with it and that it was close to what he remembered. Marty didn't remember that we used bombs and thought we had only rockets. Paul thought we had saved the centerline rack of bombs and only dropped the out-board 750's on our primary target. None of that makes any difference at all. The main points are that we were able to follow a B-66 easily, see what the B-66 found for us to hit, and kill the Radars with what was left over from our primary target. We were normally fragged for a road RECCE after almost every mission. We were not given specific routes to RECCE, but instead, could follow what we thought best. I think that we could have cleared just about all of the Radars in the North with very little trouble in '65 by pairing up a flight of F-105's with a EB-66 for a Radar hunt AFTER the Thuds had dropped on their primary target. The EB-66's knew where all of the Radar assets were, followed their progress, and kept track of any changes. We totally wasted a great chance to blind the Air Defense System of the NVN with very little cost and no change in the number of sorties flown.

CHAPTER NINE
FIRST SAM FIRING

My best shot at the first SAM Firing on July 24 '65
starts with Paul leading the CF's from east to west
about 30 miles south of Hanoi. I can't remember what
out target had been; however, I do vividly remember
looking north from my #3, spread position on his left
wing. Our EB-66 friends had briefed us that all of the
pieces of the SAM Systems were in place, checked
out, and ready to fire about a week prior to the 24th.
There was overcast at about 5,000' with clear skies
below and 5 to 10 miles visibility. We were at about
500' AGL and 500KTS or so. I heard the code words
for a SAM Launch, 'Blue Bells are Singing, Blue bells
are Singing' on guard channel being transmitted by a
B-66 right in our area. That phrase was repeated
several times. I looked toward the direction of Hanoi
and saw a SA-2 lift off and head towards the overcast,
followed by a 2nd. I could not see what the target was,
but all hell broke out on shortly thereafter from a
flight of F-4C's from Ubon. I was briefed, or read
later that the flight had turned Guard Channel off due

to the total number of transmissions at the time. In any event, one of the birds was blown up when the missile hit and the other three all had battle damage. The CF's continued with our RECCE without mishap. All flights into what later became RP-6 were stopped.

Either the next day or the 26th, Paul came into the briefing with a clipping from the Bangkok paper that quoted a New York Times article by McNamara. The article stated that we could take out the Missiles In NVN at anytime we so desired with minimal trouble. Robert Strange also was quoted as saying that the US Military had all of the personnel that it needed and had an overage of Fighter Pilots. Paul commented that it looked like Herr McNamara was about to see what he could do to reduce the number of excess Fighter Pilots. We went on Iron Hand One on 27 July and lost 6 F-105Ds and 2 RF-101's.

The ordnance, route of flight, airspeed, altitude, and formations were all spelled out in the tasking message. Although both Korat and Takhli tried to change everything except the target, all tries failed and we were ordered to fly the piece of crap as written. At Takhli the 563rd had a SAM site and the Yakota Squadron had the 'adjoining Barracks'. Korat, I think mixed the target assignments between the McConnell Squadron and the Kadena Squadron. Our initial point was Uncle Ho's Cathouse at Yen Bai, easy to find due to the number of guns that fired straight up. We were then ordered to fly down the Red River to the Sam Sight south of Hanoi. The first flight carried 2 CBU-2, aft dispensing pods each and the next two flights carried 6 each Napalm cans centerline. All flights were to fly at 360KTS and at 50' with each flight about 5 miles in trail. There were no tankers assigned; so, we climbed to 28,000, and flew at that altitude until we were into NVN. We let down and flew below 500' until we were almost at Yen Bai and then dropped to below 50'. We did deviate from the airspeed restriction and flew at 540. The rest is history. Four birds from Korat, two from Takhli, and two of three RF-101's were shot down. Of the 6 Thuds, one pilot was picked up by a Jolly Green, two became POW's and three were killed. We lost Kile Berg from the CF's on what was our 39th consecutive combat sortie as a flight of four.

All of the rest of the Charlie Foxtrots swore that we would never again accept such a stupid order from anyone, and, as far as I know, we never did.

CHAPTER TEN
IRON HAND ONE –
HOW TO BECOME DISILLUSIONED

The 563rd was put on alert for a deployment to Takhli Royal Thai Air Force Base, Thailand in March '65. Our new Squadron Commander was Major Jack Brown who had completed two combat tours in Europe during WWII and had also flown a combat tour in Korea. Major Brown had been one of the Top Guns at Nellis for several years. The Operations Officer, Major Everett Wayne Harris, was very competent and ran Operations extremely well. Our Flight Commanders were less grounded in Tactics, since they had only recently been assigned to Tactical Fighters, but took excellent care of their flights. About 50% of our pilots had come from Tactical Fighters and four of us had between 600 and 1,000 hours in the F-105. We had about average experience for Tactical Air Command (TAC) at that time. The entire Squadron, 18 F-105Ds plus two spares, left for Tahkli on 13 Apr '65 and all except the spares, arrived after one night in Hawaii and two nights in Guam on 17 Apr (the dateline ate a day). We had 18 F-105Ds when we arrived and 24 squadron pilots. Two spares went from Guam to Yakota as replacements for their losses.

Only about 50 USAF personnel to maintain the 'USAF' side of the base for several years had occupied Takhli until the build-up for SEA started in '64. The Yakota Wing kept one squadron at Takhli for about a year. The 36th Squadron was there when we arrived. The first night we slept on the floor of the small Officers Club while we waited for the barracks to be completed. Takhli had no Operations people assigned as permanent party and had no personnel to man a command section. Jack Brown and the Yakota Squadron commander worked out a plan for a pseudo Operations section. The 563rd would run Ops on odd numbered days and the Yakota squadron would run Ops on even numbered days. It worked very well for the four months we were there. The Yakota Squadrons rotated their personnel every 30 days from Japan. We flew with almost the entire wing and had zero friction. We continued to operate without a Command Headquarters at Takhli until much later in '65.

Four pilots from the 563rd flew combat sorties the second day we were there, Major

Brown, Major Harris, Al Logan and me. I flew my first mission as number two on the wing of the 36th Tactical Fighter Squadron Commander. We had four people 'checked out' that day and the next day we four again flew with the 36th only this time as element leads with a 563rd pilot as a wingman. We had all of our flight leaders checked out in three days and were on our own. We also lost our first pilot on day three; a Captain with over 2,000 hours of TAC time flew into the ground on a Rocket pass in Laos. It was the start of a very interesting tour. We flew between 12 and 24 sorties almost every day depending on the assignments from 2nd Air Division (2AD) who had Operational Control of all USAF aircraft in Southeast Asia (SEA) until 7th Air Force (7AF) was established late in '65.

In early May, Al Logan landed from a mission near Hanoi and reported that A SAM SITE was being built about 15 miles south of Hanoi! My reply was that "The rules are that we get all of the technology, they get all the Elephants, and they're cheating." Russ Violette and I both flew to that area in the afternoon and someone was indeed building a SAM site. We went to our boss, Major Brown, and reported our concerns. Jack took a flight to the same area early the next morning and found the first of many sites. He called all of us together and told us to get a plan ready to kill the SAM and left the next day for Saigon. He returned two days later with his tail between his legs, carrying a message to not fly with-in five miles of ANY SAM site. The word was not to 'disturb' any activity because it might anger the Russians who were doing the construction. A few days later, a directive came down from 2AD ordering everyone to not over-fly or disturb any SAM activity in North Vietnam (NVN). The penalty for noncompliance would be courts-martial.

Takhli received a squadron of EB-66 aircraft in May who had the mission to track all electronic activity in the North. The EB-66 had four Electronic Warfare Officers (EWOs) in each bomb bay with downward ejection seats that kept track of any and all electronic emissions. It was an underpowered, old, clunky aircraft, but they did a hell of a job that has never been properly recognized. Our B-66 friends kept track of the SAM and all other Radar activity and reported daily the progress in building missile capability in the North. We continued to receive directives not to bother the Russians. The number and activity of the SAMs continued to increase.

My Flight Commander, an Edwards Test Pilot type with almost no operational time was killed on a mission in Laos about this time. His replacement was Captain Paul Craw, AKA Charlie Chicken Expletive-deleted, one of the very best, most aggressive, natural Fighter Jocks ever born. Paul was a firm believer in flying with the same people every mission. He was mean enough and strong enough to make it happen. D-Flight became 'Charlie Foxtrot' Flight and flew 39 consecutive missions together. For those missions, Paul Craw was lead, Kyle Berg was Two, I was three, and Marty Case flew as four. We grew to be very competent, totally confident in each other, and were sure that Charlie Foxtrot Flight was the meanest SOB in the valley.

The reports from the B-66 EWOs convinced us that the SAMs were ready to shoot at any time. By the first week of July '65, the EWOs announced that all of the SAM component systems were operating, had been checked out, and were fully operational. At that time 2AD issued a code phrase to be used when a SAM was being launched, 'Bluebells are Singing'. They also reiterated the ban on any attempt to take out the threat. To say that we were nervous is an understatement.

On July 24, Paul was leading the Charlie Foxtrots south of Hanoi after having hit a target nearby when I heard a B-66, on guard channel, saying, "Bluebells are Singing, repeat, Bluebells are Singing, south of Hanoi." I was on Paul's left wing looking north and saw a Guideline Missile, followed by a second, lift off and climb into the clouds at about 5,000 feet.

The Russians had finished the checkout of their systems. The target for the SAMs was a flight of F-4C aircraft from Ubon that were in close formation penetrating the weather. The F-4 flight had switched off guard channel and was hit with no warning. One aircraft was blown away and the other three were badly damaged. The damaged birds managed to make it back to Udorn and land. It is amazing that all were not lost. The missile is 20 feet long, smokes along at almost MACH 3, and has a 500-pound warhead.

The restrictions on hitting SAMs remained in effect and we were restricted from flying within 40 miles of Hanoi. This was a totally stupid reaction that deserves to be questioned by anyone with any knowledge of the use of force. Two days later Paul brought a clipping from the Bangkok paper quoting McNamara. The main point was that "We can take out the Surface-to-Air Missile systems at any time we desire." The quote also contained the coordinates of two sites. In the same article Dr Strange stated that we had too many fighter pilots and that we should reduce the number. Paul commented on the article in rather foul language and pointed out that a good way to reduce the number of fighter pilots was to print where they were going. We also couldn't understand why TWO sites when only one had fired.

I was told that a message was delivered to the South Vietnamese Headquarters by DOD directive on July 25 that listed, in detail, two SAM sites to be attacked, date and times, route of flight to and from each target, ordnance, speeds, and altitudes that would be flown. Since anything given to the South Vietnamese would be in Hanoi in hours, I am convinced that any such directive constitutes at least Dereliction of Duty, if not Treason since 2AD, and everyone else in Saigon, knew of the leaks from the South Vietnamese HQ.

About 0600 on July 27 1965, I felt a hand shake me awake and tell me that I didn't need to get up for my scheduled mission brief since I was now on Iron Hand One, the first SAM raid. I pretended to be asleep for as long as possible to be cool and then went to the CRUB for a breakfast martini with Paul. We left for INTELL as soon as we could and found the mission order. It was the absolute most incredible bunch of crap imaginable. The 563rd was to hit a SAM site, the one that had fired a few days earlier, using three flights of four F-105Ds in trail with only one minute spacing between flights. The ordnance listed was rear-dispensed bomblets (CBU-2) dropped from 50 feet and at 360 knots. My Grandmother knew more about targeting than that! The next two flights were ordered to carry Napalm and also drop from 50 feet and 360 knots. The idiocy of

DOD was now apparent to all. If you tell anyone that you are going to hit him, and then give him almost a week's notice, any half-wit can figure out that the place will be empty and/or well defended. To over-fly an extremely well defended complex at 50 feet and 360 knots is a suicide order. The Japanese had better sense when they sent out their Kamikaze. To exacerbate an already insane order, have all aircraft fly at the same altitude, airspeed and attack from the same direction, with close intervals. I may have been a Slick Wing Captain, but I certainly knew better that that. HQ USAF, HQ PACAF, and 2AD all passed this load of excrement down without demur. I had been taught that you were supposed to, or at least try to, keep some of your troops alive. This is the Light Brigade all over again.

We truly bitched, whined and moaned. Major Brown got on the horn and tried to talk to Saigon at least three times. The Yakota Squadron Commander also gave it his best shot, all to no avail. Korat called as well. What we asked was to change the ingress and egress, change the altitudes, and increase our drop speed to at least 500 knots. At no time did we ever request not to hit the site. We were ordered to go as directed WITH ZERO CHANGES! The 563rd was to launch 12 aircraft to the SAM site. 12 aircraft from the Yakota squadron were to hit the 'Supporting

Barracks'. Korat had the same order for a SAM site and support area less than five miles from ours. The Times-on-Target (TOT) for both sites was the same and the directed routes to and from insured that we would be almost head on with the Korat aircraft. It appeared that DOD also tried to schedule a mid-air collision.

We realized that we could either comply with this stupid order or mutiny, so we went to the squadron and briefed the insanity. Major Brown led the first flight, Major Harris led the second, and Paul was leader of the last flight. All of the wingmen were volunteers. Paul never spent much time on routine details and this day his briefing was very brief. He said, "Well, we're going to takeoff with four. I wonder how many will land? Let's look at the photography and figure out what the hell we might be able to salvage." Jack Brown stuck his head in the briefing room and told us to screw the airspeed restriction and to hold 540 knots from our letdown point to the target. We completed what little we could and suited up for the debacle. We were not happy campers.

Tahkli was most fortunate to have an outstanding Chaplain, Father Frank McMullen. Father Mac started the Takhli tradition of blessing, complete with sprinkling, every aircraft that took off anytime day or night. This day Father Mac, who often attended our briefings and flew with the B-66 guys, came to the line and blessed each pilot before takeoff. He climbed up the ladder of my Thud just before start engine time and gave me absolution along with his blessing. I was raised as a Methodist and was definitely not used to a guy wearing a shawl to either bless or absolve me. I decided that I needed all the help I could get and was truly thankful for the gesture. We launched on time and headed north.

We flew into central Laos at 28,000 feet and then let down below 50 feet above the terrain, held 540 knots, and headed for our Initial Point (IP), Yen Bai, on the Red River. In July '65, Yen Bai had more guns than Hanoi; yet, it was a mandatory checkpoint in the tasking message. DOD strikes again. Paul did not over-fly Yen Bai since Paul is at least as smart as a chicken, hit the Red River below 50 feet and started for the target two miles back from the second flight.

Almost immediately we started to have 37MM flack burst directly over our flight path. 37MM guns do not have a fuse that will detonate on proximity, ergo; all of the rounds had to have been manually set to detonate at a fixed time after they were fired. The time corresponded with the expected range from gun to target. It was absolutely obvious that they knew we were coming and at what route. The reason that the 37MM rounds were high was that the guns could not be depressed any more. We flew either down the Red River or over its edges for about 40 miles, always with 37MM bursting over us. When we hit the confluence of the Red and Black Rivers, we left the river and flew over rice paddies for the next 25 miles to the SAM site. A B-66 took a picture looking down on one of our flights and it was leaving rooster tails in the paddies. We started to take hits from small arms and 50-caliber equivalent Automatic Weapons as soon as we left the river. I was hit 12 times between the IP and target, all 30 and 50 caliber equivalents. As we neared the SAM site, we came under fire from the 37MM and 57MM weapons that had been brought in to protect the site. We counted over 250 37mm and 57MM guns and a horde of Automatic Weapons around each site when we finally got the post-strike photography. Korat's experience was similar to ours. We underwhelmed them a ton. I saw what looked like a Missile propped up against a pole and a couple of huts in the cleared area of the site when we were about a mile out. There were no vans or other service equipment normal to a SA-2 site. Surprise, Surprise, it was a dummy site! It was hard to see much since Jack Brown's flight had hit the area with eight CBU-2s with all 19 tubes dispensing bomblets. Major Harris' flight had dropped 24 Napalm cans. We dropped 24 more cans into the mess. As our first flight hit the target, Walt Kosko, flying TWO, was hit, started burning fiercely, and only made it back to the Black River before he had to punch out. As I dropped, I saw Kyle Berg's aircraft on fire from in front of the inlets past the 'burners. The aircraft slowly pulled up, rolled right and went in. Marty Case, who had gone through Cadets with Kyle, called "Bailout, Bailout" and then "No way, he went in!" Paul started to pull up through a hail of bursting flack to cover Kyle and both Marty and I yelled at him to stay down and get the hell out of Dodge. Paul stayed on the deck, accelerated to 600 and wheeled for the Black. I found out in 1973 that Kyle was hit just as he pickled off his Napalm, burst into flames, and ejected. He went out at 50 feet, 540 knots and blew several panels in his 'chute. We passed Major Brown as he was trying to CAP Walt's parachute and dinghy in the Black River. He ordered both Paul and Major Harris to go home. He alone stayed to see if Walt could be found for 30 minutes, went out to a tanker, and returned for another 30 minutes, still all alone. Walt was never recovered.

We stayed low past the Black and then climbed to 35,000 and flew back to Takhli. For the first time in my life, I completely lost all control of myself. I bawled, raved, beat the canopy, and totally acted like a fool. I have never been so very angry. Luckily, I could put the Thud on Autopilot and indulge my childish behavior. I finally got myself under control about the time we crossed back into Thailand. In the meantime, I heard various radio calls indicating that Korat had lost four F-105s. We had lost at least two Thuds and at least one F-101 RECCE bird was down. We actually lost eight aircraft in less than three minutes, six F-105's and two F-101s, all for dummy targets that had been listed in the New York Time a week earlier. All of the Thuds lost were on the SAM sites. Of the 24 F-105s from both bases that attacked the SAM Sites, we lost five of the six pilots flying #2 and one leader. I was so damned angry, I was spluttering. I am still almost as angry as I was then.

Kosko, Farr, and Bartlemas were all killed. Berg and Purcell were alive, captured, and spent an eternity in Prison. A Rescue helicopter picked up Tullo from East of the Black River and took him to Laos. I'm not sure what happened to the RECCE drivers. To drive the spike in a bit further, Kyle told me in '73, after he was released, that I had rolled some Napalm under him before he hit the ground. I had a major problem with the Thud losses that day. The F-105 community was so small that we either knew the drivers or knew someone who knew them. Jack Farr had been in the 8th Squadron with me for three years. Kyle and Walt were at Spangdahlem the same time. Purcell was from Louisville, my hometown, and Black Matt and I had been friends for over two years. It was a very bad day at Black Rock.

Paul landed at Takhli with three Charlie Foxtrots and we counted holes. Of the twelve 563rd aircraft that went on the mission, two were shot down, nine had multiple holes and only one was not hit. My aircraft, 169, had 12 holes and was one of only four flyable aircraft in the squadron had the next day. When I parked my bird, the first one up the ladder was Father Mac. He handed me a French 75, slightly warm, and blessed me again. I told him that if he ever came up my ladder again, I would jump off and abort. He laughed, kissed my forehead, and said, "It worked, didn't it? Be thankful!"

I joined Paul and Marty for an INTELL debriefing and noticed that the Intelligence folk seemed to be afraid of us. We were on a short fuse and irked at everyone. We grabbed a jug of 'Old Overshoes', mission whiskey, from a poor Lieutenant and waded through the debriefing. We then went to the squadron and covered the mission taking the Old Overshoes.

How do you debrief an insane mission? Paul said that he would never again allow anyone to dictate such a stupid set of rules. Marty and I agreed. I promised myself that I would never, ever allow anyone, regardless of rank, to waste so many folk. I owed it to the people I flew with to take better care of them than that. Every one of us would have volunteered to go on a mission to whack SAMs. To be thrown away by idiots is another thing. I flew my second tour as a Weasel and never allowed anyone to put my flight in that kind of a bind. Rank or position cannot excuse incompetence. I decided that being promoted mattered much less than caring for my troops. What was anyone going to do to me, make me fly to Hanoi?

It has been 48 years since I flew on Iron Hand One and became disillusioned with my own service. I have tried for all this time to determine what went wrong. It is commonplace for Senior Officers to blame everything on Robert Strange. That is the cheap way out. Iron Hand One came down from DOD as a package. McNamara's band planned it by using a book that listed the probabilities of each weapon to kill a SAM complex. All they looked at were the estimated probability of kill for a SAM site for a long list of weapons. They chose the ordnance that gave the best probability of kill. It computed to be 99.999999% for the numbers and types they selected. Zero thought went into routes, altitudes, vulnerabilities and all of the things that even a Captain must consider before planning a trip to the head. I am not apologizing for McNamara, he was a conceited ass; however, where were the USAF Staff people when they received that mess? Not one person ever fell on his sword, not one Flag Rank ever acknowledged that they didn't question the order for Iron Hand One, and no one ever paid any penalty for those names that went on the wall. My own service showed that they cared more for their careers than for the troops in the field. The General Staff and the Flag Ranks below the Pentagon with Command Authority were derelict in their duty to us. They continued to act the same way for at least the next 10 years. I hold the majority of my own service's Senior Officers from that era in contempt. They did nothing to help the combat aircrew. The seeds of the change in the way the USAF operates today all started with Iron Hand One.

I do not include *all* Senior Officers in that indictment. In '67, for example, Takhli had Colonel John Giraudo, Colonel Larry Pickett, and Colonel Bob White as the Command Section and they were all devoted to their men. Colonel Robin Olds at Ubon had a Command Section equally as good. I doubt that there could be any better examples any time. Seventh Air Force in Saigon was a whole different kettle of fish. As far as I know, very few there ever tried to understand the world we lived in. Until Colonel White went down to run the 'Out of Country' shop, no one in the section that planned the strikes in the North that had ever been to North Vietnam.

Two of my best friends, Al Logan and Russ Violett, both graduated from the USAF with Two Buttons (Major General) and both worked their rears off to make a difference. Korat produced some outstanding folk as interested as anyone in making changes. Captain Chuck Horner flew on Iron Hand One and later did his second tour as a Weasel at Korat. I cannot speak for General Horner, but I remember Captain Horner and Major Horner. He was as adamant as I am about the duty owed to your troops. The Gulf under Lieutenant General Horner was a far cry from Korat and Takhli under 2AD in '65 or 7AF in '67. General Momyer was not at all like Chuck Horner.

General Momyer is an excellent example of my thesis. The fighter community bitched constantly about "Bomber Generals" and "Bomber Mentality." Momyer had flown fighters and had been a POW in WWII in Germany. Look at his actions. While he commanded a Fighter Group he tried every way possible to have the Tuskegee Airmen grounded of their race. Benjamin O. Davis finally got that stopped. When he was in the Pentagon he worked very hard to have guns removed from all fighters because they would not be needed. When he Commanded ATC he stopped most Formation Training, especially Tactical Formations, because they might raise his accident rate. When he Commanded 7AF he raised pure hell for more training by Tactical Air Command (TAC) for the troops being sent to SEA and at the same time did nothing to relieve us from the "Same Time, Same Route" orders being sent out daily. When he Commanded TAC he caused all dissimilar Air-To-Air to be eliminated from all Training Syllabi in use in all of the RTU units. In '68, I was sent from Nellis to defend the Air-To-Air training and was told by Sundown Wells, Momyer's hatchet man that General Momyer was going to reduce his accident rate and was convinced that the restrictions would work. I replied that the loss of the training would increase the combat losses from both MIG attacks and bombing since the training in question was necessary for both missions. Wells reply was that those could be counted as Combat Losses and I had better learn to keep my mouth shut since General Momyer was only interested in his accident rate. So much for needed training when General Momyer was not at 7AF. That is not Leadership. It is callous disregard for the Fighter Community and indicates a lack of integrity and no comprehension of ethical values. Momyer was not by any stretch a leader. I'm not sure of his Management skills either.

I am sure that the deep-seated feelings of any single officer matters little; however, I am speaking for a significant portion of a whole generation of officers that distrusted their Senior Commanders. We had some very good Leaders. Most were only Commanders and Managers rather than leaders. The workers in the squadrons distrusted most of them. Very few of the senior officers had the stature of Robin Olds.

My generation provided the nucleus of dedicated Officers that led to the Gulf and today's totally different Air Force. It does matter to have the Jocks trust their seniors. In '66, McConnell had over 30% of our troops leave the USAF after their first tour in SEA. Why? The men were very tired of duplicity, lack of support, and cover-up of munition and fuse problems. The biggest problem there was lack of leadership at the squadron level. The squadron that replaced the 563rd had 15 of the 18 pilots that made it back render their resignations for that very reason.

I still am saddened and disillusioned by the first SAM raid. I only hope that enough people will remember that debacle and work to eliminate the self-serving mind set that caused it to happen.

CHAPTER ELEVEN
TARGETS

The major problem with Rolling Thunder from day one was that the targets we were assigned made zero sense. There was never any logical sequence to the assignment of the targets. There was also no Strategic or Tactical sense to our targets at any time. In '65 the Vietnamese started to build a series of SAM Sites and we were forbidden to touch them or even to overfly any of them until after they fired at us and shot down an F-4. All of the MIG bases were also off limits until the summer of '67. We were forbidden to attack any aircraft operating from those bases until they were airborne. The targets we were ordered to strike seemed to be random selections. The Ships unloaded SA-2 Guideline Missiles at Haiphong and we could not attack them until they were at a SAM Site that had fired. We had Bridges for a while, then railroads for a while, then road cuts, etc, etc. I think my Mother could have done better than McNamara and Johnson did at the Thursday breakfast where the story was that they picked our Targets.

In '65 we were sitting in what passed for a Club at Takhli at the time. Capt Russ Violette who was a bit smarter than the rest of us remarked that he had figured out what were the most important Targets in The North. Al Logan and asked what caused that statement. Russ asked   where all the guns were.

We yakked for a while and decided that they were around the Steel Mill, bridges, a few in Hanoi and mostly around the dams, dikes, and irrigation system branch areas. Russ stated that they obviously knew what was most important and put their guns there. It seems that the only times that Vietnam was defeated was when the Chinese came down and destroyed the irrigation system. No control over water distribution, no rice. No Rice, no army. No army, surrender! We went to our boss and he went to 2nd AD. They got back to us and told us it was a Courts Martial offence to hit a dam, dike, of irrigation ditch. We never hit the single most important set of targets in the country.

In '65 we could fly over Hanoi with only a few guns shooting at us. They only had a few MIGs and NO SAMs. In '72 when we finally bombed Hanoi, there were about 15,000 37mm and larger guns in the area, 20 SAM sites, and a bunch of MIGs. We could have reduced Hanoi to rubble in a few days in '65 with few, if any, losses by the BUFFs. In '72 we lost 19 the first week of Christmas.

In 1966 the Thai Nugyen Steel Mill, which was a good target, became a primary target after being forbidden for over a year. Both Takhli and Korat were assigned two Alpha Strikes each day for each base for a week. The Smelter area was the first target and although it was destroyed on day one, the attacks on the Smelter continued for a week. All other parts of the complex were Verboten. The next week we were sent after the rolling mill only. This was followed by a full week of the loading and transportation docks. Each was destroyed on the first day. During this time they built up their defenses until the Steel Mill was more defended than Hanoi! The real problem was that the Steel Mill had squat to do with the Vietnamese ability to wage war because all their war materials came down the railroads or through Haiphong. The vast majority came through the port of Haiphong. Although Haiphong was a Navy Target for years, the ships were never hit nor were the harbor mined until the Christmas bombing of Hanoi in '72.

Each F-105 Base was ordered to hit two Rolling Thunder Targets nearly every day with almost the same take-off times and target times because of scheduling the Tanker support. If weather was so bad we could not bomb North Vietnam, we were given targets in the Lower areas of the country or Laos. Sometime we were sent to work with a Forward Controller (FAC) instead. In '67 all Alpha Strikes (Rolling Thunder missions in North Vietnam) had three assigned targets, a primary Alpha Strike, a secondary target of less importance, and a dump/FAC assignment. All three were planned and briefed until we were executed to a target from the list. With luck we would get the execution word as the mission briefing was starting, if not, we waded through the whole mess. Since the morning briefs started at about 0300, life got tedious. An Alpha Strike consisted of four 4/ship flights of bombers and one 4/ship flight of Weasels. The MIG CAP consisted of a 4/ship flight of F-4s. With luck we would get we would get Olds Flight from Ubon with Robin

Leading.

In '67 at Takhli the Order (FRAG) came in daily in the afternoon for the following day. With luck the FRAG would come in by 1600 and the Mission CC for the mission would bring his planners to the Command Post and plan for each of the Targets. Once that was done the package was turned over to the Battle Staff and they would have a folder complete with maps for each pilot ready for the morning go. The afternoon go was planned in the morning and the briefing would be about 1300. In addition there were several daily non-Rolling Thunder targets in Laos picked by 7th that were planned by the flight leaders assigned for those missions as soon as the FRAG Broke. Typical Alpha targets were Bridges in or near Hanoi or a defended railroad near there, selected targets in Hanoi such as the Thermal Power Plant, one of the MIG bases, or a munitions/fuel dump. All of the Targets in the Hanoi Valley were extremely well defended. As you got out of the Valley the defenses became less intense; however Kep Airfield was almost as bad as down town Hanoi. The planning sessions for the Hanoi area were intense to say the least and sometime lasted for over an hour.

With two Elephant Walks (Alpha Strikes) every day, it was amazing that Maintenance could cover the load. They never missed a mission. I think that the best way to describe the time was that everyone was very tired and a bit grumpy. We had a young Capt in the 357th who became a mission Commander on his 49th sortie. Nealy Johnson was a slick wing Capt from

ATC and became one of our very best. In the end of Oct '67 to early Nov '67 he was Mission Commander 10 consecutive days and never had a mission outside of Hanoi. Brother Nealy was a very tired Fighter Pilot!

To repeat myself, Rolling Thunder was the worst use of Air Power since the invention of lift. The thing to remember is that this went on from mid '65 until late '68 with only a few pauses. In Aug '66 Takhli and Korat lost a total 27 F-105s. That was over one Squadron of the six in SEA. I think that the term 'Operational Tempo' was very high and the results were not worth the effort. Our Pilots and Line troops busted our rears for all that time and came home to a volley of jeers.

CHAPTER TWELVE
TARGETING AND TACTICAL PLANNING

After '65 almost all of the normal Squadron or Wing Tactical considerations disappeared into 7th Airforce (7AF). The daily tasking (FRAG) came down in such detail that there was little left for the operational units to plan for. Refueling times and tracks caused us to, more and more, use the same routes, formations, and Attack Tactics day after day. This coupled with the lack of recent experience by the unit commanders caused a tactics vacuum in all our thoughts. When I arrived at Takhli in May '67, we went the same way almost every day using the pod formation and almost the same ingress and egress routes time after time. We also had a policy in the 355th Wing that RANK LED! Unfortunately most of the ranking types were not very good at any type of flying and most needed two or three Seeing Eye Captains to get them to the target. It was a mess. We started to improve when Col. Bob White became the Deputy for Operations. We had gotten to the point that everyone understood the 'Pod Formation', how to fly it, and how to use it to keep the SAM's off our backs. That and the more aggressive Weasels cut the SAM losses way down;

however, we still had a real lack of realistic daily planning.

The severe lack of experience in combat planning coupled with an equal dearth of Tactical flying skills was the root of all of our problems. From the end of the Korean Conflict until the early '60's, almost all of our fighter squadrons were used as little SAC bombers and about all we knew how to do was fly low level, sit alert for nuclear response, and throw bombs over the shoulder. There had been very little preparation for any conventional operations either Air-To-Air or Air-To Mud. All we had in the inventory were WWII left over bombs and fuses that we obsolete at best. In addition to all those problems our Flag Rank Officers were un-ready and/or un-fit to conduct conventional operations. The only people that had even thought about real Tactical Operations were the Fighter Weapons School at Nellis and a few very unpopular warriors who had not forgotten what combat was really about. The vast majority of our line fighter pilots and an even larger percentage of our Squadron and Wing Commanders were unready for SEA. The higher up the Command chain, the less the staff and Commanders understood what was needed to fight in SEA.

An example of a very basic consideration that demonstrates our problem was what airspeed to carry when we were in areas where we could be attacked by enemy aircraft, missiles, and guns. We found that if we kept our ingress airspeed above 540 KCAS and our altitude below 10,000', our MIG-21 problems virtually disappeared. By starting to increase indicated airspeed and decrease altitude as we crossed the Black River, The MIG intercept became much more difficult. By having the MIGCAP trail our 16-ship POD formation about 3 miles or so. The MIG-21 either had to cut in front of the F-4 MIGCAP or run out of gas trying to catch us from a 5-mile trail. The missile seeker on the MIG had real problems picking up a target when it was being carried at high airspeed below 10,000'. A simple increase in ingress airspeed coupled with about a 6,000'/8,000' altitude cut our probability of losses to MIG's to almost nothing. The F-105 could stay in the high threat area as long holding about 540knots as we could holding 450knots because we had to use much less afterburner to accelerate when we had to really maneuver. The magic altitude to remain above was 4,500' to stay above the AAA and 37/57MM flak. It seems an obvious thing to do; however, it took over a month to convince some of the RANK of the obvious. Most of our senior officers had never even thought about airspeed and continued to use peace-time thought processes instead of looking at the problems of combat. The real LEADERS, as contrasted to the Managers, understood and adapted quickly.

Our use of the very clumsy Pod Formation was a real problem as well. The Electronic Jamming Pods that arrived in '66 were not very effective, required lots of care and feeding, and required that we fly in a very clumsy almost line-a-breast formation with a 500 to 750 foot separation from each other coupled with a

200 to 300 foot altitude stack. A single Pod by itself actually created a better target return for the SAM Radar although it did deny them range. All they had to do was line up the AZ and EL returns and keep the missile on that line until it hit the Pod. The four-ship formation caused at least 16 points of intersection and cut way down of the effectiveness of the SAM system. When we flew four flights of four in a double line 8 wide and 2 deep each flight holding about the same distance from each other and each aircraft holding the same altitude and space staggers, the SAM basically stopped being a threat. It was worth the effort to fly that clumsy SOB to keep the SAM's off our backs; however, it really caused problems of maneuverability and left us very vulnerable to MIG attack. As our experience level grew, we learned to space the F-4 MIGCAP in trail with the sixteen-ship strike force, increase or speed, lower our altitude, and tough it out until after we had split into 4 separate flights to drop our ordnance. It all worked and our loss rates dropped to less than half by mid'67 when compared to early '67 or '66.

A continuing problem that was never adequately addressed was the severe lack of experience of the replacement crews sent to SEA as the old TAC aircrews completed our tours. The decision was made that 'Nobody goes back until everyone has done one tour'. That was a stupid decision based on the ridiculous idea that all pilots were alike regardless of what they had been flying in the past. There is zero way to take a bomber pilot or a transport pilot and put him in a fighter after a six-month school and have anything approaching a competent driver. The quality dropped like a rock and the impact sent loss rates up again. Not only were the pilots new to the business, the Squadron and Wing Commanders were also unqualified to Command in combat. All of this causes impacts on the Tactics that can be flown, on over all accuracy of the bombing, and raises losses. The capabilities of the pilots drive what Tactics can be flown and what Tactics are too difficult for the pilots to handle. All of those problems have been written about by knowledgeable folk since the end of the war.

One of the last things to be discussed is Ordnance and Fuses. In '65 we didn't have squat that worked and we were stuck with un-safe weapons and fuses that caused losses in both people and aircraft. By the end of the conflict we had very good weapons and fuses that fit our requirements. In addition we had laser-guided and electro/optically guided weapons that really changed our Tactical considerations. If you can put munitions within a foot of where you want it, you don't need very many aircraft or bombs. The caveat to that is that the weapon must have the penetration and blast to kill the target you are after. The Than Hoa Bridge is a perfect example. We started bombing that sucker in'65 and never took it down until '72. I have watched multiple hits followed by more hits with M-117 (WWII 750# bombs with only damage to the roadway and the bridge still standing. The M-117 just couldn't take out the piers. If we had been given the MK84 (Navy 2000#) bomb, we could have taken out the piers in '65. The losses would still have been bad due to the requirement to get close to the aim-point to get a hit; however, we could have taken it down. In '72 we had the MK84 with a laser guided nose package and could take it out from 15,000' with very low risk. All of the Tactical considerations change as the ordnance and fuses change.

CHAPTER THIRTEEN
TARGET PLANNING AT WING LEVEL

In '67 there was virtually zero real Target Planning at Wing level. The Frag (fragmentary order) came down from 7AF daily with all of our targets, times on target, number of aircraft, Ordnance, Fusing, refueling tracks and times, and a Partridge in a Pear Tree. This left us with only how we would conduct ourselves in the target area. Ordnance selection and fusing is extremely important for any target, unfortunately, we were given ordnance and fuses that were in the bomb dump, not what would best take out a target. The folk in Saigon really didn't have the foggiest idea what was **_required_** to kill a specific target or what could be best delivered for best aircrew survival. There were NO Weapons School Graduates in that Frag Shop. We mostly had WWII ordnance such as M-117 (750lb.) bombs, M-118 (3000lb.) bombs and old fuses that were either WWII or Korean. The only new bombs were the Navy developed MK. Series and they were in very short supply. They were MK81 (250#), MK-82 (500#), MK-83 (1000#) and the MK-84 (2000#) bomb. We didn't have any fuses that were designed to use the penetration capabilities of the MK series weapons. In addition, the only new bombs at Takhli were the MK82, or Ladyfingers, that had too little explosive to really kill most targets. We had gotten a few Mk-83 and MK-84; however, they were gone and the company that made them was on strike. We really didn't have much to work with. This was not the best of all possible worlds.

The old M-Series bombs were designed to be carried by WWII Bombers and really wouldn't penetrate any serious distance into a hard surface. You can't crater a runway unless you can get a bomb to go through the concrete and then detonate. If you only manage to make holes in the surface, the runway can be repaired in a matter of hours or days. If you put a MK84 (2000#) through the runway surface and detonate it several feet below the hard surface, you make a crater several feet across and make repairs much harder since the subsurface must also be dug out, refilled, packed, and refinished before you can repair the hole. Bridges are similar in that you must be able to penetrate into the support structure to bring down the bridge. You may hit the roadway and even take down spans; however, as long as the support structure is standing, the bridge can be repaired in hours or days. The M-118 was a Block Buster with all blast and zip penetration capability. The weight was 3000lbs with 2000lbs of explosive. The case was very thin and could only penetrate soft surfaces such as dirt. If you dropped it on a concrete surface, the case would rupture and the explosives would go low order even if you had a fuse with a sufficient delay. The M-117 weighed 850lbs and had about 450lbs of explosive. This gave a bit more penetration capability but not enough to make any difference. Both the MK117 and the M-118 were also very old with most dating from WWII. The explosive was starting to separate and neither bomb could take much shock before it would explode. As bombs age, the explosive starts to separate from the filler and pool in the cracks just like dynamite. In '68 we ran a test with un-fused M-117 bombs at Nellis and had over 75% of 100 drops explode on contact when dropped on a dry lakebed. Both of those old bombs were not safe to carry.

Fuses were just as much of a problem. Most of our fuses were designed for carriage by bombers in bomb bays. They were all mechanical (clockwork) with a propeller on the fuse that would turn a certain number of revolutions and then arm the fuse. The fuse was designed for speed of no more than 300knots. Our normal drop speed was about 540knots. The fuses would either fail or arm almost as soon as they separated from the bomb rack. They were not safe to carry. All of the newer fuses are electronic rather than mechanical. It sounds as though just we may have had a few problems.

In July of '67, Col. John Giraudo, AKA the Great Kahuna, called Sam Adams and me into his office for a chat. He had seen a new list of possible targets that were being considered for strikes. He was very interested in one that was the Air Defense Center for

North Vietnam. It was in a park almost in the center of Hanoi near a Lake (the same lake where McCain landed in Oct). My hold baggage was rifled when I left Takhli and, among other things, all of my notes were stolen; so, I'm not sure of the dates or even the name of the complex, I think it was the Bac Mai Military Center. I know it was built by the French and consisted of three bunkers with 24"; steel reinforced concrete walls and safe doors, covered with 15 feet of overfill. All that was visible from the air were the mounds of dirt above the complex. The Wing King asked Sam and me if we would work up a plan to take out the headquarters. Both Sam and I were Weapons School graduates and both were Weapons Officers for our Squadrons. He told us that he was very interested in getting this target for the 355TFW. He urged us to work as fast as we could and to specify numbers of aircraft, ORDNANCE, and FUSES. He wanted to take a completed plan to 7AF and present it to Gen. Momyer with a request to be given that target. Sam and I went to work as soon as we were dismissed.

We got into the books and quickly determined that only a MK84 with a delay fuse could penetrate the over-burden and get into the bunkers. If we could get any bunker penetrated, it would cease to function and all of the folk would also cease. There were no fuses at Takhli, any other base in SEA, or even in the States, that would allow us the delay times required. I remembered that Nellis was testing a new electronic fuse, FMU-26, that was supposed to have a long delay. I got a call through to Nellis through the Command Posts and found the action Officer. He told me that the fuse had failed the test and was being redesigned for several problems; however, the delay function worked like a charm. The problem was that only the setting was a 26-second delay. I asked him to find out if the MK84 could take that long a delay and to find all of the FMU-26 fuses and hide them. Sam found where all of the MK84 bombs in SEA were hiding and started to have them sent to our bomb dump.

We called each Squadron and had them give us a list of their best bombers and a guess-t-mate of their accuracy. Sam and I figured that, One: if we could get the MK84s, Two: if we could get the FMU-26 fuses, and Three: if we could name the best bombers, THEN we had a good chance to kill the target if we had a minimum of 12 aircraft carrying two MK84's each. We found exactly 27 MK84 bombs in all of SEA and started them our way. 27 MK84 bombs equal 13 ½ aircraft loads at 2 per aircraft. I got the call from Nellis that the MK84 could take a 26 second delay with a very good chance of penetrating into the bunkers and that they had about 100 FMU-26 fuses. I had them all flown to Takhli ASAP. We had every one of the top bombers at Takhli volunteer for the mission and passed their names to our Deputy For Operations, Col Bob White. Sam and I left the Command Center about 22 hours after we started. We also requested, and later got, F-4C RECCE photography of the complex at about 1400 hours

Hanoi time to give us the best chance of seeing the shadows cast by the bunkers. The shadow patterns were very important if we were to be able to see our aim points. The last thing we did was to brief Col. 'G' and Col. White. They said "Good Dog", patted our heads and sent us to the bar. We were a bit sleepy after two plus days with no sleep and spent a short time in the bar for a change. Col. Giraudo went to see Gen. Momyer. In the next couple of weeks the MK84s and FMU-26 fuses all arrived at Takhli and we received the RECCE photography we had asked for.

About a month after we had planned the Air Defense strike, I landed from the morning mission to Hanoi after leading the Weasels and was met by Sam Adams. The scheduled afternoon Mission had been changed after we took off for the early mission to the Air Defense Headquarters and ALL of our planning was included. I had very mixed emotions because I wanted to be on that one and could not go because only one mission a day was the rule and it was ALWAYS enforced. Sam Adams got to lead the Weasels. We had specified two flights of four, one north of Hanoi and one south, and we got them! Bob White was the Mission Commander and _All_ of the Aircrew in the Force were from our list of Volunteers. I do remember that Dale Leatham led Bear flight. We had 12 aircraft with MK84 bombs with FMU-26 fuses set at 26-second delays and four aircraft with six CBU-24 bombs each for the guns. Ubon furnished our MIGCAP. I think Robin Olds was MIGCAP lead. The short version of this is that we got everything we had planned for.

I went to the command post and listened to the mission radio calls during the mission for the first time ever. This was a bad idea since it made me very nervous; however, we made it in and out with no losses. Post-strike strike KB-70 cameras showed that we had hit every bunker. Our best estimate from the strike photos was that we had all but five MK84's hit a bunker, that's 19 of 24 hits! The pilots really had a super day. I have seldom seen happier guys than that debriefing. We had really nailed an important target using the right ordnance, the right fuses, and the right people. It was the only mission I ever saw that was planned properly from the first. I still wonder how many fewer people we would have lost and how much better we could have bombed if the mission planning had been properly done.

About a month later Col Giraudo called Sam and me into his office to sit in on a special Intelligence briefing. We had some airborne assets that listened to all of the Air-Traffic from North Vietnam. The voices had been mostly identified and what control functions each had. The frequencies were being monitored when we hit the Command Complex. All transmissions from the Headquarters ceased at the same time and none of those voices were ever heard again. In addition, there were no MIG attacks for three weeks, and the SAM activity dropped by more than half. We really did hit them where it hurt. If we had gone with our usual loads, I doubt that the facility would have even been damaged and I'm sure that they would have beefed up their protective systems. I may only be bragging; however, it sure helps to do it right the first time. If you happened to notice, Chuck Horner took out the Air Defense Control Capability on night one at Baghdad. It helps that Chuck was a Weapons School graduate besides being very smart.

CHAPTER FOURTEEN
KEP AIRBASE – A WORTHWHILE
TARGET...BUT

I think everyone had a target in North Vietnam that they hated. The one I disliked the most was Kep. It was on the Northeast Railroad from Hanoi to China. It was Northeast of Hanoi about 100 miles or so. It was also Northwest of Haiphong about the same distance. The Town of Bac Gang was near, the Bac Gang bridge on the railroad was very close, and the turning Y that was at the junction of the Northeast Railroad and the Rails that ran to Steel Mill was even closer. All of this added up to some 1,200 37mm and larger guns to shoot at you.

Kep didn't have as many SAMs around but the ones that were there were very good. The area was flat with no hills to hide behind and they had good Radar coverage from the time we crossed the coast to the target. In addition the gunners didn't have to figure out which Target we hitting since they were all so close together. The last problem was that to get there from the west you had to over fly all of the defenses in the Hanoi Valley. That was not good!

The mission order always included the refueling

track and that was always either Brown or Tan. Those were the Water Tracts over the Gulf of Tonkin. The route to the target and back was to fly from Takhli to just north of Danang, turn left and find your Tanker. The track paralleled the coast to the drop of east of Than Hoa. We then went North of Haiphong well off the coast and turned in to hit an Island that had the Kam Pha Mines where they shot at you. It did make it easy to find because there was 80mm and 100mm flak hanging over the place. From there we would fly about 15 minutes to Kep, bomb it, and head back the way we came.

The big difference of operating north of Haiphong was that it was a long way to an area where the Jolly Greens hung out. The USN Big Mother Choppers were charged with Rescue and they were on a boat. There was no way they could get up North of Haiphong in less than two hours. In the parlance of the time, it was Dog Squeeze! If you ever pick up a Poodle by the neck to speak to it, you will know what Dog Squeeze consists of!

The last truly bad part of Kep was that the average mission was some 6 ½ hours minimum. Long missions, less chance of rescue, a large bag of guns that were very accurate, SAMs, MIGs from there and Hanoi and the long distance to our tankers after the mission made Kep about as welcome as a dose of Clap in a nunnery! My personal view was that I would rather eat Dog Squeeze with a spoon than go to Kep.

CHAPTER FIFTEEN
A TYPICAL MISSION IN 1967

Scheduling, planning, and even some tactical considerations were different between Korat and Takhli because Takhli chose to assign the Wild Weasel crews to each squadron. Korat instead kept all of the Weasels in one squadron. There are strengths and weaknesses in both systems; however, I am partial to the Takhli method. That is based on my observations from 15 May until 2 Dec 1967 as both a Weasel and Strike pilot in the 357th Tactical Fighter Squadron (357TFS). The reason for my preference is that I was able to fly with our own Force Commanders more often. Since the Force Commander was selected from each squadron, I was able to really get to understand those from my squadron and to help them understand how the Weasels could best support them. Being familiar with the Mission Boss's mind set paid great dividends.

Each squadron in the 355th Tactical Fighter Wing (355TFW) had five flights instead of the normal four. E-Flight was the Weasel Flight in each squadron. The E-Flight Commander was normally the ranking

Weasel and was also, normally, the Route Pack 6 (RP-6) Weasel Flight lead for his squadron. I was E-Flight commander in the 357TFS as a Captain and usually had at least one Pilot and always had an EWO who ranked me. I did have the most combat and total Fighter time. This seemed to be enough for the 357th Commander to name me to command his Weasel Flight. I kept the job until Carlo Lombardo; my Electronic Weapons Officer (EWO) went to Saigon with Colonel White, our Wing Deputy for Operations (355TFW/DO) in Oct. I was assigned D-Flight Commander until I left.

I scheduled my folk to fly on a daily basis by giving an updated list to my Operations Officer each day for the next day's flights. I led almost all of the RP-6 Weasel missions given to the 357th. In addition to the crews directly assigned to each squadron, all Wing Staff Pilots were attached to a squadron for flying duties. My squadron, 357TFS, had Col Bob White, assigned as well as two very good folk from Standardization and the Wing Weapons shop. Everyone was needed and everyone was used. We always seemed to be short handed. We periodically were short of RP-6 qualified Weasel Leaders in the wing. We would often be asked to furnish a flight lead, an element lead, or a wingman. This happened quite often early in my tour and I flew with all three squadron and almost every Weasel in the wing. We did not fly with other EWOs. I would rather share my toothbrush than share Carlo. We flew as designated crews unless we were short of two-seat aircraft and had to fill in with F-105Ds. We later had some very experienced strike pilots volunteer to fill in when we were short handed and had to use F-105Ds in the Weasel flight. It worked extremely well.

Takhli and Korat both were scheduled for two Alpha Strikes each day. Alpha Strikes were those flown into RP-6, the Hanoi area. An Alpha package normally consisted of sixteen F-105D, single seat aircraft, loaded with bombs and four F-105F, two-seat aircraft, for the Weasel support part of the mission. Each Alpha package also had four F-4D, two-seat aircraft from the 8th Wing at Ubon or the 366th at Danang. Although there were variations of this scheme, over 90% consisted of sixteen F-105D strike aircraft, four F-105F Wild Weasels, and four F-4C MIGCAP. The targets, ordnance, refueling tracks, times, special instructions, and a Partridge In A Pear tree were all sent out daily in what was called the FRAG.

The FRAG, or Fragmentary Order, was a huge thing that arrived each day electronically to the Communications van sometime in the afternoon. If we were lucky, the FRAG would arrive by about 1500 and if not, we were stuck with a late session planning for the early morning launch. It took about an hour for the CRYPTO folk (code breakers) to "Break" the Frag apart and hand the portion that applied to us to our Operations staff. On a normal day we would get a call that the FRAG was in and ready by about 1630.

The responsibility for each Alpha Strike rotated

through each of the squadrons in the wing. The squadron responsible for furnishing the Strike Commander also, normally, furnished two flights of four F-105Ds strike pilots and one flight of four F-105F Weasel crews PLUS one spare for each flight. Each of the other squadrons furnished one flight of four F-105D strike pilots and a spare. That worked out so that any given squadron had two days of responsibility for planning and leading an Alpha Strike in a row and then had only to furnish one flight for each Alpha Strike on the third day. Of course, there were also missions assigned each squadron every day for Laos and the lower parts of North Vietnam. Maintenance would assign aircraft, including spares for each mission as soon as they could figure out how many flyable aircraft were available in each squadron. They did an absolutely wonderful job and all of the ground personnel worked incredible hours to keep us in the air. You were usually able to fly your assigned aircraft or, at least, a bird from your own squadron. When we had been hurt badly, we were assigned what was available from any squadron.

The planning for an Alpha Strike started as soon as possible after notification. The Force Commander would take those folk he thought he needed, or wanted, down to the Wing Operations Center and look at what was on tap for the next day. The first mission was usually a very early launch. Mission briefing for the crews was seldom later than 0400 and normally earlier with a takeoff time of 0530 or so. In order to be ready for the 0330 briefing, the dawn patrol was planned the day before. The afternoon go was planned the morning of the mission starting about 0900 and, except for the time of day, was like the dawn patrol missions. After a break for chow, the briefings would start.

The Mission Boss, Force Commander, would look at the target the included instructions and ask for comments from his picked guys. The planners almost always included the Weasel Flight lead and at least the Deputy Force Commander. Each Mission Boss had his individual way of planning and of obtaining advice. The good ones always asked for advice, especially contrary positions. The key to any mission was the quality of the planning. The best way to have the loss rate climb was to assume that anything was easy and that we could repeat what had been done before. We kept a BIG book that held a debriefing of each mission stressing what was good and what was not for the mission flown. Smart folk really paid attention to the book. Once the Mission Boss had decided his plan for the next day, the Worker Bees with him would draw up a map, fill in the mission cards with the pertinent information, and hand them to the super staff in the Ops Center. They would prepare all of the materials for each member of each flight and have it all filed in slots for the 0-dark-30 briefing. The planning could take from one hour to several hours depending on the target, the thoughts of the Mission Boss, and the phase of the moon. Each mission consisted of a Primary Target, a Secondary Target, and a Tertiary, or dump, target. All were planned for each mission. When planning was over, the planners could go to the Officers Club and relax with a fifth of Scotch and a pitcher of beer. How else can you sleep after looking at all of the bad things planned for your body the next day?

Carlo and I had a ritual that we went through for every trip to RP-6. We would walk the walls in the Ops Center. The walls of the planning area were lined with very detailed maps and photography. Several very detailed maps of the Hanoi area were kept updated daily ranging down to 1 to 20,000 scales. The photography was updated as often as possible and was printed in the same scales. If you walked slowly about six to eight feet from the walls, it was like looking at the ground from 4,000 to 10,000 feet altitude. We would walk along our projected route of flight and visualize the actual ground. We would check for any markers that would lead to suspected SAM sites, locate the most numerous gun pits, and try to memorize what we would be seeing the next day. This would continue for at least an hour every time we planned a mission. Even if I had not been scheduled to lead, Carlo and I would walk the walls. I was not nearly as senile as I am now and could remember what I had visualized. We had points to hit in order to loft Shrikes at each site, references to find each SAM site, offsets in order to roll in the flight and bomb a given site, and, lastly, not be surprised if every thing turned dark brown. When you play 'You Bet Your Rear' there is never too much preparation.

The area around Hanoi was a circle with all sorts

of strange restrictions. It was colored a bilious shade and had lines and markers in red, pink and green. We went to one early morning coffee klatch, and a friend, Gary Olin popped up and said "Jesus, the damned thing looks like Sparkies' EYEBALL!" and it stuck. Carlo and I were invited to Ubon to give a Dog and Pony show for the 8ᵗʰ Wing and Colonel Olds introduced us with this comment, "If you wonder where Sparkies' Eyeball came from, come look at these orbs."

When the evening stroll was completed, we would repair to the Takhli Club for attitude adjustment. The Club was our home. If I had ever acted the way I acted at my lovely Lady's abode, I would have been shot. The CRUB was home there and it was a fairly rowdy place. Mostly it did allow us to let off what passed for steam and forget what was on tap for the next day.

My alarm would wail at about 0230 or so and I would shower, shave and leave the trailer I shared with Carlo and walk the fifty feet to the back door of the Club in 15 minutes. Breakfast was quick and we would be at the Ops Center in a very short time. The morning briefing always started with a time hack and a word from our favorite weather guesser. Stormy would pull out his crystal ball and give us his very best guess for the target area. INTEL would follow Stormy and then the Mission Boss would start his brief on the Targets. If we were lucky, the WORD would come in telling us which target we were going after. If not, the Mission Boss would brief all three. The Ops Center would deliver the WORDS. Each target had a designator word with an assigned code word for success, a code for SAMs, a code word for MIGs, etc. These designators were the WORDS. Every activity has its own silliness and that was ours. The Mission Briefing took maybe thirty minutes. Once we were committed, i.e. sent to a target, the Mission Boss would finish his pitch, and then each flight, including the spares, would head for their own squadron and conduct a flight briefing. The flight brief covered procedures, bombing tips, MIG look out, RHAW (Radar Homing and Warning) items and/or what the flight commander wanted to cover. Most briefings were brief. The average briefing lasted thirty minutes or so. If you had an NEWBIE (New Guy) the brief could push the walk time.

Once the briefings were over, everyone tried to have a few seconds alone before donning his flight gear. When the flight was suited up, the squadron Pie Van would drive you to your aircraft. By the time you had put on your G-suit, helmet, survival vest, guns, knives, parachute, survival radios, lucky charms, several baby-bottles full of water, etc, you had added about ninety pounds to your weight.

The Crewchief would meet you with the aircraft forms and hold your flashlight so you could read them and sign the release. Preflight was normal given the darkness and it was very normal to have a flightline supervisor show up and follow you around. This was their way of showing you, and the Crewchief that they cared about each pilot. I have never seen better-maintained aircraft anytime, anywhere. I can't say enough about our wrench benders. They worked incredible hours and gave all of their effort to the aircraft.

Start engine time was when the pace really started to increase. We used a big shotgun shell like charge about the size of a two-gallon jug to start the big bird. Black smoke would roll and the engine would wind up in about thirty seconds. All checks followed in sequence and about 95% of the time, all five in a flight would be ready to taxi in sequence. The Alpha Launches were called Elephant Walks by the folk. The flight line would go from silence to bedlam in less than a minute. The first aircraft to taxi were the five or six KC-135 Tankers (Boeing 707 full of gas) for a take off about 20 minutes before the fighters.

The last two flights in the Strike Force would taxi first, followed by the Weasels, and then the Force Commander and the second flight. The order was caused by the Refueling cell arrangement. The last two flights and the MIGCAP refueled on the high cell while the Weasels, Force Commander, and 2nd flight had the low cell. The take-off sequence allowed us not to fly through another flights altitude block. We would have all twenty-five F-105's following each other like a circus parade out to the arming area at the takeoff end of the runway. If you really wanted to look like an elephant walk, you could extend and retract the refueling probe. Weapons were armed and the four primary birds for each flight would take the runway together. Runup was followed by single ship takeoffs at 10-second intervals. The burner plumes of each Thud lighted the night as it accelerated to takeoff speed. As soon as one flight took off, the spare for that flight taxied to the far end and sat in the de-arming area until released by his flight leader. The next flight would pull into the arming area and the cycle would continue.

After all the Force was launched, we would head to the Refueling assembly point. The refueling tracks were named for colors. The one used most often for our trips to Hanoi was Green Anchor. Green track ran from about 180 miles north of Takhli into northern Laos. The Anchors were the ends of the tracks. The KC-135's would join up with the low cell of three leading them at about 17,000 feet altitude. Each aircraft in the cell was stacked up 200'. The high cell took off first and was based at 19,000. The low tanker cell refueled the Weasels on the lead tanker, the Force Commanders flight next, second flight next. The high cell was only about 5 miles in trail and refueled the third flight, forth flight, and the MIGCAP. Each flight joined with its tanker and initially took only about 1,000 lbs. of gas just to check the system. Occasionally we would take two or four spares along to the end of the track where, if no one needed a spare, they were released to a Mission in Laos.

About forty minutes prior to our drop point, I would start the refueling cycle. We always refueled Lead, Three, Two, and Four, in that order. It takes five or ten minutes to completely fill up from the airborne gas station and the order cited insures that the wingman have the most fuel at drop off. Wingmen always use more fuel than the leader or element lead since they have to maneuver more to stay in formation. After #Four finished, I would jump back on and top off, followed by the rest of my flight in the same sequence. We would continue this dance at shorter and shorter intervals until we were only taking about 100 to 200 lbs. We could hook up, sip a bit, unhook and have the next guy on the boom at less than 30-second intervals. When we hit the drop point, Barracuda always had maximum fuel in every bird. There is no such thing as too much fuel.

When we dropped off of the KC-135, the Mission really started. Up until then, there was always a chance that you could be recalled or diverted. After drop off, you were committed to go Downtown. The Weasels were supposed to be 'First in and Last out" on every mission and we were with few exceptions, since it was best for the Force to have us out in front and sniffing for SAMs on the way in. The best place to be on the way out was trailing the force five miles or so to insure that Mr. SAM couldn't jam one from six. The MIGCAP worked best when they trailed the Strike Force by five to ten miles. This caused the MIG-21, our worst airborne threat to have to pull in front of the F-4's missiles to get a shot at the Strike pilots.

The distance that the Weasels would be in front depended on several factors. How many MIGs were we to expect? What was the weather? How obstreperous were the SAMs going to be? How good were the Weasel Crews? What did the Mission Boss want? All of these things had been thrashed out in the planning phase an agreed distance had been decided.

The sixteen-ship Strike would form up in a gaggle of four separate flights that actually were a single jamming package. Each flight flew with all of the aircraft about 750' apart (no less than 500' and no more than 1000'). This allowed the jammers to overlap each other and create a huge blob of jamming coverage on the enemy Radar screens. The Force Commander would fly as smoothly as possible since all four flights were cueing from him. The #2 flight would move into position about 1500' out and almost line abreast from his lead on the side away from the planned roll-in direction. His wingmen would fly the same formation as the lead flight. #3 flight would fly in trail about 2000' back from lead and the #4 flight would fly behind the second flight. We called it The Gaggle or 'The God Awful Formation' and even though it worked and cut down tremendously on SAM losses, we still hated The Gaggle. It was very hard to maneuver and really cut down on our ability to look around for attacking enemy fighters.

The clumsiness of the formation caused us to fly in straight paths more than anyone liked. Since there is really no free lunch, we did the best we could and flew the Gaggle since it did keep down the losses from SAM missiles. The Weasels didn't carry any jammers because they would jam our receivers. We would go blind to the threats if we turned on a jammer mounted on our own aircraft. A jammer also took replaced a Shrike. I would much rather carry a Shrike than a jammer that only worked in formation. Think of it as having a very sensitive listening device that can hear whispers at 80 miles and then having Led Zeppelin start to play ten feet away. We only existed to protect the Strike force and couldn't do it if we used the jamming pods. The Strike package would join up in the briefed formation with the Weasels in front and the MIGCAP in trail and head for the Barrel.

As we crossed into North Vietnam we would "Green 'em up, Music on". When the gunnery switches were ALL set to dispense ordnance, the station buttons would light up Green i.e. "Green 'em up". The jammers were a kind of music and we always wanted to be escorted into the Barrel by a band. We still were, in many ways, an elephant walk. The normal distance for the Weasel Flight was five to ten minutes ahead of the force. This allowed us to root around and stir up the SAMs. Once we got them on the air, we could play games with them and place ourselves in position to best cover the Strike package.

We needed to be between the Force and the main SAM threat when the Force broke formation and started their dive bomb runs. They were very vulnerable at this time since a single jammer didn't help against the SA-2 system. They needed all the help they could get until they were able to get back into overlapping jammer formation. Another trick the bad guys tried was to fire missiles, especially from behind the Force to get them to break formation. By being several minutes in front, the Weasels could also give a weather report to the Force Commander. An accurate weather report would allow him to change the direction of attack, change altitude, or even abort the mission if the weather was really foul, before getting into the nest of SAMs that lived in the Hanoi area.

The real high threats started at the Red River. We tried to keep the speed of the whole Alpha Package at or above 540 knots from short of the Red River to target and back to the Red. This speed cut the threat from the MIG-21 by over 50%. In addition, the shorter time you are in range of any gun, the longer your life expectancy becomes. Once past the Red River, the SAMs and guns multiplied at a great rate. The area around Hanoi, the Barrel, had over 12,000 37MM and larger guns, up to eighteen SAM sites, and two MIG Bases. This was in an area about thirty miles in diameter, about the size of the Las Vegas valley. It was a bit like being in hell with your back broken.

As we approached the pool table flat ground near Hanoi, the Weasels would double back and set up a much closer coverage of the Force. The MIGCAP would move out of trail and cover from a flanking position. The radio would get very noisy if we weren't careful and radio discipline was always a problem. One of the jobs for the Weasels was to 'Call Threats'. The EWO in each Weasel would keep a running commentary about the electronic threats around us and discriminate valid missile launches from spurious ones. They could tell if the indication was valid, where it was coming from, and who was being fired at with a fair degree of accuracy. Only Barracuda One made all threat-warning calls from Barracuda Flight. Calls of "Shark Force, disregard the Launch Light, Barracuda heads up, it's at us" were common and helped the Strike Force when they were at their most vulnerable. The call the Force did not like was "Heads up Shark, It's a valid launch from Lead Nine!" At least they would know where the missile was coming from and that it was aimed in their direction. The Weasels would try and have at least two Shrike ARMs lofted towards the SAM sites that were the worst threat to the Force during their dive bomb run. The Shrike homed in on the Radar energy from the SAM Radar. If the SAM driver kept emitting in order to guide his missile, the Shrike would hit his antenna. To stop the Shrike from hitting him, he had to shut off all power to his Radar and abandon the Missiles in flight. Very seldom did the SAM site stay on the air and risk both their Radar and their own rears.

If we could find a SAM visually and if the situation allowed, the Weasels would dive-bomb it using our cluster bombs. It only took one of the eight CBU's we carried to total the site. They did not want that to happen, so they were very cautious. The Guideline Missiles were kept fueled. The propellants were Kerosene and Red Fuming Nitric Acid and are hypergollic. If only one softball sized bomblet of the over 500 in each CBU hit near a missile; it would ignite, run around on the ground and explode. The vans were equally vulnerable and a hit would kill the site and the folk. The whole idea was to make the

SAM drivers nervous and shaky. Nervous and shaky folk are prone to not taking good shots at our folk. When the Strike Force rejoined and started out, the MIGCAP would fall in a staggered trail to cover them and the Weasels would trail every one out of the barrel. Happiness was re-crossing the Red River.

The trip home was much easier since we were almost impossible to chase down from behind and the Weasels were in position to hammer any SAM stupid enough fire at the Force. The Tankers would be waiting at Green Anchor Extend in Laos with fuel for anyone who needed it. We would climb to a good cruising altitude of about 30'000' where we used much less fuel and it was cold. When we were in RP-6, we normally kept the air conditioning system shut down to inhibit smoke and fire coming into the cockpit in case of a hit. The cockpit temperature would be well over 120. We were expending energy at a great rate, drenched with sweat, and everyone had a mouth full of cotton as we crossed the Red. Happiness was the cold water behind the headrest of the ejection seat. The 450 miles to Takhli was very easy and allowed time to determine what had happened that was good and what could be done better the next day. The trip home was an excellent time to rate our individual and group performances. It was also a very good time to go on autopilot and get rid of the whips and jangles from all of the stress.

The entire Force of twenty F-105s would arrive at home base at nearly the same time. The ground Crew all would stop and count the birds as we came down initial and broke for landing. If they counted all of us they were very happy, if we were shy of that number, the faces that came up the ladder were very grim. The ground crew took every loss as a personal affront. We were always marshaled out of and into the revetments with a salute and a big grin. The Crew chief would hook the ladder onto the cockpit and almost run up to hand us a cold washcloth and a very welcome cold beer. They would bring up our Aussie Outback hat and take the helmet. Their first question was about the mission and the next was, "Can I turn her around". We would go to maintenance to debrief the aircraft for any discrepancies and then head for the squadron and rack our flying gear.

As soon as possible we went to the INTELL shop at Wing Ops and sat through a detailed briefing. The Force Commander would normally have the Strike Flight leaders and the Weasel lead meet him for a very quick debrief and then we would 'Put It in the Book' for the next planning session. A debriefing at the squadron followed for each flight to determine how we could do better and to ensure that anyone who had messed up learned not to do THAT again. After this last debriefing, the Mission was over and we could go to the bar. The Mission really lasted about a day for the Force Commander and the planners. It was a short ten hours for the line jock that flew Four, NO hill for a stepper.

The next day, we would do it all over again. In June of '67, I flew 24 Wild Weasel Combat Sorties and was scheduled every day. Six missions were canceled for weather and I led on 22of the 24 that went. I had 18 sorties in RP-6 of which I led 16. In my spare time, I flew seven test hops. I logged 107.5 hours that month. I had never logged over 45 hours in a single month in my life. The typical Thud Driver at Takhli was tired and needed rest. To quote Tom Kirk, Commander of the 357TFS "All you have to do is hurl your butt at the ground 100 times, and then you can go home and peck crap with the chickens". That summed it up as well as anything.

CHAPTER SIXTEEN
CREW COORDINATION
LOMBARDO & SPARKS 1967

Crew Coordination is the single most important part of being a Weasel. Nothing can be done unless the information available in the backseat is transferred to the front seat. Carlo Lombardo, my bear, used to bitch that 'All the brains are in the backseat and all the decisions are in the front seat'. He was right. Carlo had over 20 years of experience as a EWO and I could only spell Electronic Warfare with help. Carlo had zero experience in Fighters and wouldn't recognize a Tactic if it bit him. I had a shade over 2,000 hours of fighter time, 1,000+ in the Thud, and had 63 combat sorties in '65 at Takhli. The reason the Weasel birds were built was to allow a EWO to determine what Radars were in the area and what they were doing. The gear in the backseat was clumsy, hard to use, and required complete concentration by the EWO. The only gear available in the front seat was the APR-25/26 (later APR36/37) that was in all the F-105s in Thailand. The resultant was a requirement for both cockpits to talk to each other in such a manner that the Pilot could understand where the threats were and what they were doing. That was a tall order and was the root problem for all Weasels.

Carlo and I started to understand what was required shortly after we started Weasel School at Nellis. We both had problems with what items were important, when they were important, and how to understand each other. By the time we left Nevada for Thailand, I knew that Carlo was the fount of all knowledge and he trusted me not to fly into the ground. The day we got to Takhli we, of course, went to the Stag Bar first to settle in. Jerry Hoblit and Bear Wilson were celebrating their 100 Mission Soirees. Jerry and I had spent 3 years together in 'D' flight, 8TFS, 49TFW at Spangdahlem. Jerry and the Bear left their party and spent the rest of the night telling us how to stay alive in the North. It was the best lesson we ever received and it worked.

We flew our first Weasel sortie June 1, '67 as #2 in the Weasel flight led by Maj. Bill Campfield that covered a strike near Phu Tho. Carlo and I floundered around like beached fish for about 30 minutes. We saw our first SAM in flight, shot two Shrike Missiles, saw a bunch of flack, and managed to get out of the area alive. After we finished the debrief we went to the 357th and spent over an hour trying to determine what we had seen, what had happened, and what we had to do to add to the mission and not add to the problem. We went from there to the Ops Center and spent over two hours walking the walls looking at photography and annotated maps. We were trying to build mental pictures of the brown stuff we had waded through that early morning. Carlo was trying to visualize what his scopes would show and what the angular relationships would be as we maneuvered in the threat footprints. I was trying to form a mental picture of where the threats were from various easily seen features on the ground. The first day trip around the Ops Center walls became a daily ritual for us.

The next day Carlo and I briefed for a 0-Dark thirty mission near Phu Tho in RP-6. Since we were way short of F-105Fs, I flew as #2 in a 'D'. I spent another 30 minutes flailing around on the Campy's wing dumber than a sack of rocks. I fired two shrikes from a close wing position, saw a lot of flack, no missiles, came home, and debriefed. Carlo and I then went back to the Ops Center for another two+ hours. The next day Carlo and I led the 357th to RP-6. No SAMs, lots of flack and no loses. By the end of June '67, Carlo and I had flown 22 combat sorties, 16 of which were in RP-6. We led 14 of the 16 RP-6 missions Weasel Missions. I flew an additional 2 missions in a 'D' in RP-6. Of the 6 missions outside RP-6, we flew four of them as BUFF support night missions in the lower routes. I had 24 combat sorties and 7 test hops in June for a total of 107+ hours of flying time. We were both very tired.

By the end of June, Carlo and I had gotten our communication (read crew coordination) down fairly well. We found that the key was to prepare for each sortie as completely as we could. After each mission debrief, we'd go the Ops Center and walk the walls looking at what was annotated, what was right, what was wrong, and what we had actually done. When the Fragmentary Order (FRAG) came out, Carlo and I would start to prepare for the next days mission. If we were on the dawn patrol and were lead, we'd meet the Force CC at the Ops Center the night before and help plan the mission. After the routes had been decided and the over all plan was firm, Carlo and I would walk the walls for at least an hour and then head for the club. If it was a PM launch, we'd do everything the same except it would start in the morning. The key to all our planning was to walk the walls and build the best picture possible every mission. It may be possible to Weasel without all that work; however, we always tried to be as prepared as we could be. I have heard that it is possible to get laid in a MG; however, a motel is a lot better.

Crew Coordination is more a mental process than a rule driven thing. Carlo and I worked on the principle that he had all the information, he said brains, and that I had the best picture of the real world. He was responsible for giving me a picture of what threats were there, what they were doing, and who was shooting. I was responsible for taking that knowledge and applying it in real time. As he said, he had all the brains and I had all the decisions.

In order for the Nose Gunner (Billy Sparks) to make a decent decision, the Pitter (Carlo Lombardo) had to build me a picture of what was happening in real time in ALL threat bands. The picture is best built in segments. After we dropped off of the Tanker, Carlo would start by checking the number and types of long range detection Radars. BARLOCKs were of special interest since they directed the MIGs. Height Finders were next for the same reason. In '67 there were only two BARLOCKs in the country and when neither one was operating; MIG-21's were seldom seen. Height Finders were also closely associated with MIG-21s. If we had both BARLOCK and height finder activity, MIG-21 Company was very likely. If neither was on the air we never saw a Fishbed. The MIG-21 threat was very important to the types of formation we could fly. No 21's, we could easily split into pairs and not worry about the MIG-17s since we NEVER flew slower than 500 knots. If Mr. Fishbed decided to play, the flight needed to stay somewhat closer together.

While we were still far from the fray, Carlo would start counting the number and direction of the Gun-Layer Radars. If we had a bunch of Firecans looking at us, we could expect more SAM activity since the Gun-Layers could track the Jamming package of the 16 Ship Force. No Firecans when we were way out, lower SAM probability. As we got closer to the Valley, Carlo would drop the acquisition Radars and start to pick up the threat emitters. By the time we were about to enter the Hanoi Valley area, he had dropped everything but Gun-Layers and SAM Radars. Once when we had 16 SAMs on at the same time, he dropped all Firecans and all SA-2 radars that were less than two rings. Carlo did have all the brains and I was stuck with all the decisions.

All information was passed vocally between

cockpits. The way Carlo and I worked was for him to continuously transmit his view of the Electronic world to me. He would start by building an overall view of the arena to include the probability of MIGs. He would go from there to his best guess of the SAM threat. He ended up with only the information about the threats that could touch us. I think that he could hit peak gusts of several thousands words a minute when the cheese became truly binding.

I very seldom said anything to him until we had to go into attack mode for a Shrike launch or to attack a SAM site with hard ordnance. If I needed to reply, I'd shout "SHUT IT" and be as short as possible. In our airplane I made all the outside radio calls. Takhli had tradition that all 'Launch Lights' were verified by the Weasel Lead. When the Launch Light came on, Carlo would check it against the other systems and make a validity call only to me. I would then call the force or flight with a 'Valid launch' or 'Disregard the Launch Light' call. He would then continue to update my picture. After we got our stuff in a sack, he knew what I was going to do and what to tell me. I could read his grunts and groans rather well. The best thing in any mission was for Carlo to say "Going Cold Mike". That meant that we were out of the area headed home and he was about to hibernate for a while.

Crew Coordination in all of the housekeeping functions of flight was simple. He owned the Weasel Gear and the Doppler and I owned everything else. Carlo had little interest in navigation and told me that if he had wanted to be a damned Navigator he would have become one in '42. I informed him that I sure as hell didn't need any help flying or navigating and that worked for us. I offered to teach him how to fly, refuel or other cockpit tasks and he flat didn't care. It worked for us. Most EWO folk wanted to learn how to fly to some degree and several, Mike Gilroy especially, could do about anything a pilot could. Carlo, Grouchy Bear, did what he wanted and it was fine with me. Crew coordination should be unique to each crew in some degree. The only thing that matters is to protect the Force and KILL SAMs.

How any Weasel crew best manages to relay information from the EWO to the Nose Gunner is right for that crew. I flew with several Bears other than Carlo and each was different. I highly recommend our method but I know that each pair must fine tune a system that works for them Each Crew is unique to themselves and there is no master key to information transfer. I was very fortunate to have Carlo and to be able to stumble on a methodology that worker for us for 47 trips downtown. The important part is that the environment drives the requirement. If it works, it's good. If it doesn't work, the crew will probably not be around very long.

The bottom line is that, for us, Crew Coordination was simple. Carlo was in charge of keeping me informed of what the threat was likely to be each mission, keeping track of where the threats were, and what they were doing. He told me when a site was about to launch and what his friends were doing. He verified every launch light to me. His only duty other than the Weasel gear was to keep the Doppler under control. I owned all Tactical decisions. If I wanted to shoot a Shrike at a signal, I'd tell him to line me up. If I decided to attack a Threat with hard ordnance, he'd keep me informed of its friends. I made all Radio calls and did all of the Navigating. To repeat, Carlo had all the brains and I had all the decisions. It worked for us and we had a total of 5 photo confirmed SAM kills.

CHAPTER SEVENTEEN
SHRIKE LAUNCH PLANNING
LOMBARDO & SPARKS 1967

Carlo and I arrived at Takhli a bit after dark on May 15 '07. We flew in on a Tanker with Col Bob White who was going to be the new 355TFW/DO. We arrived at dark, got set for the night with a bed, and went to the bar. J. Noel Hoblit and Bear Wilson were celebrating their 100th mission in great style. They left their party and spent the rest of the night trying to transfer a tour's worth of smarts at one swell foop. Both stressed the importance of Shrike Envelope Recognition and the equal importance of being able to arrive at the right point in space to give the best probability of hit. They really stressed loft parameters and how to arrive at the proper release point. We listened and started to learn as much as we could about the Shrike. It wasn't much, but it was all we had and was a very important tool to keep the SAM driver's head down.

Since I owned all of the front cockpit knobs and switches as well as the bombs, bullets, and missiles, it became my job to put us in the right climb angle, direction, and airspeed to give the little bitty missile it's beat chance. In order to do any of this both of us had to have the best idea of where the SA-2 batteries were hiding and where they were in relation to each other. There was a humongous list of VN's listed in our target books. A VN was known position surveyed and prepared to receive guns and SA-2 missile systems. A VN was used when any of the threats were repositioned. SAMs were repositioned very often except those very close to or inside Hanoi. The problem was always to know which VN's were occupied.

An occupied VN was then known as a Lead and had a number added to allow INTELL to plot the suckers as they were identified. Takhli was very fortunate to have two squadrons of EB-66 aircraft that spent about all of their time flying around with several EWO's looking at scopes and working at determining where each of the SAMs were. We also had the Weasels plot what they saw after each mission and the mission planning boards were updated after each Weasel or EB-66 was debriefed. The end result of this was that MOST of the SA-2's sites were plotted very accurately. The further from Hanoi you went the less likely the information became. Close to 'Downtown' we knew where the bastards were most of the time accurately enough to launch a Shrike with a good chance of getting a hit.

The biggest problem was to figure out which of the Leads was up and ready to shoot. If the Weasel EWO could tell the Nose Gunner which one was up, the Nose Gunner could then head for it and set up for a shot with a Shrike. Carlo and I 'Walked The Walls' (the boards with all of the information were on the walls) before every mission for at least one hour to burn in our minds where each of the Leads should be on the ground and what the angular relationships would be between each of them and our position at anytime in the Hanoi area. I would pick out an easy spot to recognize on the ground and then memorize a heading from that spot to a Lead. I used 600 KTS ground speed to compute a time in seconds to start a pull to a 20, 30, or 45 degree loft for a shrike. If all went fairly well and the Tactical situation allowed, Carlo would identify a Lead that was locked on or looking at us or the Force and identify it by number. "Lead 21 is left 30 locked on with 2 ½ rings" I'd pick out my reference point, and head for the site at 600 KTS. After the right elapsed time I'd pull to the loft angle and either launch, or fake a launch, depending on the situation. This allowed us to increase the number of shots that hit by a very large bunch. Carlo and several of our EWO's best guess was that we were getting a bit over 15% hits. That was a big increase.

The Shrike had a much shorter range than the SA-2 Guideline Missile. The maximum range was from a 45 degree loft angle and that was about 15 miles at 600 KTS. A 20 degree loft would get you about 10 miles and 30 netted about 12 ½. The SAM operator had a problem. If he kept his Radar on, he had a very high probability of having his Radar antennae hit. If he turned off the power to the system to defeat the Shrike, his missile would go unguided and miss, plus it took about a minute to get back of the air after he shut down. The sudden power shutdowns really played havoc with his magnetrons and increased his maintenance problems by a bunch. Shrike gave us a chance to play with his mind a bit and make him nervous and that's good.

By the time Carlo left to go to 7AF in Oct, most of the Weasel Crews at Takhli were using some variant of our system. Shrikes did not KILL a site; however, they sure kept their heads down and allowed us to clear lanes for the Force to get in and out of Hanoi. Col Bob White borrowed a phrase from Carlo that he used for a while. "A 30 second spot at the Super Bowl cost about $250,000. A Shrike can get me almost 60 seconds of playtime from an SA-2 for under $25,000, and that makes it very cheap" Like all of us, I'd much rather roll in on a SA-2 and kill all of the Vans, explode the Missiles, and let the air out of all the operators, but a Shrike was also useful and satisfying in its own way.

CHAPTER EIGHTEEN
PAUL DOUMER BRIDGE
STRATEGIC & TACTICAL TARGET

Paul Doumer was a much hated French Governor of French Indo China. The main Railroad and automobile bridge spanning the Red River in Hanoi was named for him. The bridge had multiple spans with huge masonry pilings. It carried the vast majority of the material that went from North Vietnam to the south. Railroads from China, The Steel Mill, and Haiphong all used the Doumer to cross the Red. Even the railroad from western China ran down the north side of the Red and crossed at the Doumer. All Major Bridges, marshalling yards, and railroads qualified as meaningful targets, the Doumer was tops.

The interesting part of planning a strike on the Doumer was the vast number of guns in the area. It was almost in the center of the ring of defenses that surrounded Hanoi. Flack killed more aircraft. Over 75% of our losses in the North were to guns. There were over 12,000 37mm and bigger guns in the Hanoi circle. Over half of the MIGs were at Phuc Yen and some 18 to 20 of the total of 24 SAMs were in the same circle. Given this, the Guns were the biggest threat. In addition to the big guns, there were an estimated 250,000 small arms and automatic weapons as well in the Hanoi area. The small arms could hit anyone below 3,000' and the bigger but still agile 37s and 57s forced us to stay above 4500' since a Time of Flight of less than 4 seconds negated jinking as a valid tactic. If you flew straight and level below 10,000 you were a dead pigeon. If you were above 10,000' the MIG-21 could run up your butt and stick an Atoll in it. By staying above 4500' and below 10,000 and keeping the speed over 540 Cal, we were able to minimize the optical threats and the Jamming Pods kept the SAMs off our backs.

We looked at the weapons available to take down the Doumer and found that we did not have any bomb and fuse combination that would destroy or even damage the pilings. The 750s would not do enough damage and the 500s were a joke. We didn't have any 2000 pounders available since the factory that made them was on strike; so, we looked at the WWll M-118 3000# block buster bombs. After a lot of 'what ifs' we picked the 3 grinder with instant-non delay fusing. The idea was to put the bomb under the center of a span and literally to blow it up, not down. A three-grinder put out about 10+ PSI and that would lift the span off the trusses and drop it into the Red. The main problem now was being able to ignore more flack than you could imagine, fly through 2 or 3 layers of bursting rounds and meet your release parameters. We had a pure manual sight and we did pure manual deliveries. It was a lot like being in hell with your back broke.

The Pods could cover the SAM and radar directed gun threats up to pop and roll-in. From pop-up to roll-in altitude until the 4 flights were rejoined, the Weasels were charged with taking out the SAM threat. It took a very brave MIG driver to come into all that flack, plus Robin and his merry men took good care of us going in and coming out. The Weasels concentrated our Shrike shots to cover the force from the most dangerous site emitting in the area. To say that everyone was a bit antsy is a severe understatement. Brown shorts were numerous and common. The strangest thing of all was that all of our jocks looked forward to the GOOD targets and the Doumer was number one. Even a dumb fighter pilot under stood.

We hit the Doumer three times while I was there and managed to drop a span every time. John Piowaty of huge red mustache fame went on all three and dropped a span every time. The first time we got 1 span, the 2nd got 3 spans and the last got 7 of the 12 spans in the bridge. I think that target alone speaks very well of the dedication and valor of the 355th. I was Weasel lead for all 3. Understandably, I am still am very proud to have been a member of such a great band of brothers who offered themselves daily for our country. I only wish that our country understood what was really happening.

CHAPTER NINETEEN
SUNDAY MASS AT TAKHLI

One Sunday morning in July '67 during the peak monsoon period at Takhli a bunch of Dragons had just finished all the debriefs from a '0-Dark-30' mission. It was near noon and Ted Moeller was driving the Pie Van in a frog drowner downpour with visibility at 20 feet or so. He swung the Van around and told me to open the back doors and backed up to an F-105D being loaded with M-118, 3,000# bombs. Lightning was flashing and the rain looked like Noah was headed back. Father Horan was conducting a Mass for a single load crew on the ramp.

It had to be a Sunday because the Chaplains wore uniforms instead of fatigues on Sunday. Father Horan, completely drenched in his vestments had his Jeep backed up to the Aircraft. The Jeep had a small altar on the back with the load crew kneeling in the rain facing the altar waiting for the sacrament. The good Father completed the rite, gave the troops absolution, and finished as though he were in Saint

Peters. After he finished his blessing, he drove to another bird with another load crew and started another Mass. It was still pouring rain.

As Ted drove away, I remember thinking that this was the way things should be. Father Horan was tending to HIS congregation the best way he could. To this day, I still think that was one of the most memorable services I have ever seen and was the epitome of true belief and dedication to what all religion should be. To say that Father Horan was popular with the troops is a tremendous understatement.

All of us in the van were silent and had problems with our throats all the way to the Club. Once there, we repaired to the bar to have our own service.

CHAPTER TWENTY
OLDS FIGHT MIG CAP

As Wild Weasel Flight Commander in the 357TFS in '67 I was fortunate to lead the Weasels some 47 times into RP-6. On about 40 of those flights, my Force Commander was Col Bob White and Olds Flight, from the 8th Wing was our MIG CAP. For some strange reason Olds Flight was always led by Col Robin Olds 8TFW/CC. There are many things worse than having such superb folk to fly with and very few things better if you have to fly into the most heavily defended are in the world. The Hanoi Valley was flat as a pancake, over 40 miles across. It had by most estimates some 500,000 small arms and automatic weapons, over 12,000 37MM and larger guns, some 30 to 40 MIG fighters, and up to 18 of the 24 Surface to Air Missile (SAM) sites in North Vietnam. The SAMs in the valley were all up and sniffing as anyone entered the barrel. The closer you got to Hanoi, the worse it got.

One of the missions that stick in my mind was in late July or early Aug '67. Col White led Shark Force, 16 F-105D bombers, I was Barracuda Lead with 4 F-105F Wild Weasels and Col Olds was Olds Flight

Lead with 4 F-4D MIG CAP. The Target for the day was smack downtown at, I think, the Thermal Power Plant. I sped up from the KC-135 Tankers on Green Anchor in Northern Laos to get nearly 20 miles ahead of the Force with Robin about 5 miles behind me covering us from MIGs with his Radar. I crossed the Red River swung into the valley from the north for a weather check keeping my track pointed well north of Hanoi in order to keep from pointing directly at the Target.

The whole valley was clear. I stayed north of the city and then went back west to get about 5 miles in front of Shark. I came in ahead of Shark and Olds was now close in at Shark's six. This allowed Olds Flight to keep both the Force and the Weasels covered. On this day Robin split his four-ship and he covered Barracuda. As I headed back down the Ridge, several SAMs came up and started to track my flight. I split my four-ship into pairs with about 3 to 4 miles trail and tried to line up a SAM in order to squirt a SHRIKE anti-radiation missile at the SAM that would be the biggest threat to Shark. There were 3 or 4 of the suckers north of the city who were playing games by taking turns tracking me and then shutting down.

I finally got one lined up and pulled up for a loft shot with a Shrike. He dropped off the air as I started my maneuver and I really jerked the bird around and headed back toward the city. I was right over Phuc Yen Airfield. The Airfield had about 2,000 37MM and larger guns sited there. All of them seemed to be shooting at me big time. I checked over my right shoulder and saw Olds Lead at my high 5. Robin called out "Thud over Phuc Yen, You've got a MIG at your six!"

I saw the MIG-17 about a mile back out of range and since I had 590 on the clock, he was falling further behind. I transmitted "Got him Olds, I'll make him predictable" and rolled my Thud up on the right wing and really jerked the nose for a short time, then let off on the 'G', kept the bank and watched the engagement. The MIG driver bit, pulled way inside the turn and started to lob 37's at me. Since Olds Lead was high and inside the turn, he pulled his nose up, did a huge barrel roll maneuver that looked like it was right out of the Weapons School manual, over the top of the MIG-17, slid well to the outside of the turn, pulled from below the MIG to line him up for a AIM-9 shot and blew him away.

All of this was done in about 30 seconds with a slew of guns shooting at him. Robin yelled "I got that One!" I hit the mike button and wise assed a "Barracuda will confirm that as a kill! Want me to drag another in front of you?" Robin hollered "You Son Of A Bitch" This was the first and only time in my life I ever got one up on Robin! We continued our Weasel Mission and got off a couple of Shrikes at the SAMs to keep them off of Shark as they bombed. After Shark Force headed out I followed everyone out of the Pack to insure that no SAM got lucky. We hit a 57MM gun site on the way out and headed home since no SAMs would stay up long enough to allow us to find and drop our CBU-24s on it. We hit the post strike Tanker and headed home to Takhli. It was a very good mission since Shark hit the target and no one was lost.

I was in the Intelligence debriefing at Takhli over 2 hours later when a Sgt told me that I had a call of the 'Colonel's Red Phone'. I went to the battle cab and it was Col Olds. He said "You wise Ass, thanks for the confirmation. I owe you a steak at least" He was laughing and added that I also could drink free at his club anytime. Robin bought me a fillet the next time we met and I did manage to drink free at his club, house, and numerous other spots.

I have never flown with a better combat leader in my life. He was unique. He valued people for their skills and treated anyone he thought could walk and chew gum with respect. He was especially considerate and respectful of those he thought were Warriors. Rank didn't seem to matter to him. As an example, I was a very wise assed Captain and Robin was an incredibly respected Colonel Wing Commander and yet he treated me as a peer. It mattered to me when I was Barracuda Lead to be his friend. It matters even more when I am Mr. Sparks, Lt Col USAF, many years retired. I now have a much better idea of what a combat phenomenon Robin Olds really was. It took me quite a while to figure out that Robin never claimed that kill. I am sure that it was number Five at least and he only claimed four on that tour. There was never anyone better. I was honored to have flown with such a warrior.

CHAPTER TWENTY-ONE
A MEMORABLE 100 MISSION PARTY

We enjoyed 100 Mission Parties at Takhli more than you could imagine. The reason for this was because the 100 Mission Parties let us believe that there just might be a way to finish and go home. My favorite, or at least most memorable, 100 Mission Gala was in September 1967 when we had three guys from the 357th Squadron finish at nearly the same time. Big deal and big party! In addition, Father Horan, our Catholic Chaplain, was finishing a year at Takhli and was invited to the party as well. Father Horan was one of our favorite folk. He was to be found at the arming area blessing the aircraft as they left for combat missions, at the Stag Bar to minister to the needy, or flying with the B-66 folk to see what it was really like in North Vietnam. He was truly one of the good guys.

Although this was to be a Squadron affair, we invited three other Chaplains to help send Father Horan off. The Chaplains were; Chris Martin, as good a chaplain as ever lived,   Erickson, cut from the same cloth, and Father Berriger, a Jesuit replacement for Horan. Our Operations Officer, Major Jim Light, got us off the afternoon go for the day so we could start the party at about 1400 hours ROTC time at the Ponderosa. There were a few house type buildings at Takhli called the Ponderosa's, that all had a living room, bedrooms, baths, and a small kitchen. Compared to the hooches, they were palaces.

The assembled multitude hoisted an enormous number of beverages to start the celebration in great style. Ted Moeller (pronounced Molar) and I unlimbered the Banjo and led the group in song, mostly profane, but songs in any case. We kept up the merriment for 3 hours until it was time to take the show on the road. The road was short and led to the Takhli Officers Club. This was to be the Main Dining Room and not our normal haunt, the Stag Bar known as the CRUB.

We entered in normal 357th style with Ted and me leading all of us in song, "We Own This Club", as we marched, or wandered, to a table set for all 30 of us. Great glee and gusto abounded at the table. As we were served drinks, food, drinks, food, drinks, desert, drinks, etc, I noticed a Lieutenant Colonel sitting with a Full Bull who seemed to dislike our act fiercely. Said Lt. Col. was our Chief Chaplain, LtCol. Davidson was a Southern Baptist, who was noted for disliking all fighter pilots, enlisted men, and almost everyone else. The O-6 sitting with him was his boss, the Chief Chaplain from 13th Airforce.

We finally finished the food and had started our speeches for the departing 100 Mission Troops and Father Horan when Chaplain Davidson sent a note to our Chaplains. Jim Light intercepted the note and read it to the mob. It stated that it was 'Unseemly' for the ministers to be sitting with such a 'Drunken' group. As you might imagine, we took umbrage at that and stood and sang Chaplain Davidson a Hymn. A Hymn is simple and consists of, "HIM, HIM, FUCK HIM." We obviously thought that was fitting and laughed loudly. Chaplain Davidson was not charmed and came over to our table and gave our four Chaplains a direct order to leave the table. He was very angry and shouted at us as well. As our Ministers were leaving, the Fighter Pilots stood on the table and sang him another 'HYMN'. Jim Light decided that we should continue the festivities in the CRUB, where our four Chaplains had gone and, led us out singing "We Own This Club."

As Ted Moeller and I walked by the Southern Baptist's table, he made a remark that tended to make both of us even angrier. I can't remember what it was; however, anything he said would have worked. Ted and I looked at each other, put the Banjo on the floor and decided to dance on his steak. We grabbed a bottle of truly shabby red wine and poured it in his very thin hair, jumped on his table, stomped on his steak, splashed steak juice all over him, jumped down, picked up the Banjo, and went to the Stag Bar to continue the 100 Mission Party until 0'Dark Thirty.

The next morning at 0700, the phone rang in my

trailer. The Chief Master Sargent who guarded the door of the Wing Commander, Colonel Giraudo, told me I had 15 minutes to appear at the Bosses Office wearing my mess dress flight suit. I jumped in the shower, shaved and made the Wing HQ with 1 minute to spare. As I started in the door, Ted Moeller slid his motorcycle up next to me and we both asked "WTFO."

We were escorted in to see the Big Kahuna, snapped to attention, saluted, and continued to make chins. We were met with silence for a very long subjective time. The Boss finally asked us if we had done the following things. "Did you sing a Hymn to Chaplain Davidson?" "Yes, Sir." "Did you pour wine in his hair?" "Yes, Sir." "Did you dance in his steak?" "Yes, Sir." "Why the hell did you do that?" I could think of nothing to say and Ted, an Aviation Cadet who I thought was a West Point Graduate, said, "All due respect Sir, The Colonel's a Shit." We were both at rigid attention and had a problem seeing much since we were staring several feet above his head. After a while the Big Kahuna gurgled, and stammered, "I know he's a shit, but you can't dance on his steak! Get your Asses out of my office NOW!"

Ted and I saluted, did a formation about face, and, in step, marched or his door. As we started out the door we heard a thump from Colonel Larry Pickett's office, the Vice Wing Commander, next door as he fell from his chair. Col. 'G' gasped, "Larry did you hear that, the Colonels a shit!" as Ted and I left the office. The Zebra, Chief Master Sargent, was hanging on the wall, holding his stomach and roaring. He told us to become scarce since the Boss had really been mad. Ted and I became very scarce and made it to the 357th.

A few days later, the Zebra told me that Colonel "G" and Colonel Pickett spent some time together and then had the base Commander and Chaplain Davidson both come to the Head Shed for a small 'Come To Jesus' party. The outcome was that the Chief Chaplain was forbidden to talk to any of the Fighter Pilots who didn't start the conversation. He was also ordered to 'not bother' the troops. I never saw him speak to anyone in the mess or otherwise have anything to do with the troops from then until I left. Our remaining three, after Father Horan left, ministers continued to care for the troops. In retrospect, I think that my Wing Commander handled the Chief Chaplain very well. I also think that Ted Moeller and Kathleen Sparks little boy were very, very fortunate.

CHAPTER TWENTY-TWO
THE FIRST PARTY SUIT TRIP

Tom Kirk, the 357th Squadron Commander, was known for his original ideas. He was talking to Ted Moeller one day and asked if Ted thought that really distinctive Flight Suits for parties would go over with the Dragons (Our patch was a Dragon with his tongue sticking out). Ted had seen the Night Owls from Ubon wearing standard flight suits dyed black and told the Boss that that was a very good idea. Tommy, AKA the Super Ball, asked Ted if he could look into getting the Mad Takhli Tailor to make some for us that would have standard pants pockets, custom fit, and be YELLOW. Ted thought that was a super idea and took it on as a project. He had me go downtown with him and we were promised three 357th specials in less than a week.

The bad news was that Lieutenant Colonel Kirk was shot down the day before the first three suits were completed. Ted and I wore our two tailored YELLOW beauties to the club and were mobbed by every one. This started a race for Party-Suits for all of the units on the base. Red ones, Blue ones, and our original YELLOW ones were ready in a very short time. The 357th Party-Suits were covered with the appropriate patches and worn with a Black dickey. We were very sharp dudes!

Shortly after this I was shot down, grounded, and assigned the job of trying to replace Tom Kirk as the planner for the Third River Rat Party. The first had been at Korat; the second at Ubon, and the third was to be at Takhli the tail end of November 1967. I asked Ted to stick around after he had finished his 100 missions and help with the Red River Rats party. He stayed at Takhli and did an enormous amount of work for the two or three weeks we had to put this mess together. The big difference for our soiree was that we were going to take everyone to Bangkok for the Sat night banquet and super party at the Oriental Hotel.

Ted and I went to Bangkok almost once a week overnight to keep up with the myriad taskings that had to be corralled. We normally stayed at the University Hotel because it was handy to the Oriental and cheap. We decided to wear the YELLOW Party-Suits on one of the trips to check the reaction of the Thais and the management of the Oriental.

Captain Moeller and Captain Sparks caught the Klong Airways gooney bird and managed to get out of Don Muang Airport alive and unskinned and into the city. We walked into the University Hotel in glorious color wearing the YELLOW suits, Black Dickeys, Sunglasses, Overseas Caps, swagger sticks, and dragging our hang-up bags behind us. We swaggered up to the reception desk where there was a C-130 crew checking in. The Aircraft Commander (AC) was a Lieutenant Colonel wearing a Wheel Hat, a spoon in his pencil pocket, and low quarters. This may sound like a joke except that his Major Navigator was fat, wore a Wheel Hat, low quarter shoes, and had two spoons in his pencil pocket. The Rest of the C-130 crew was all there in flight suits, Wheel Hats, low quarters, etc. The Co-Pilot, Flight Engineer, and Load Master were lined up behind the AC and all had spoons in their pencil pockets.

Ted and I smoothly moved up to the counter and started to sign in. The C-130 AC looked at us, did a double take, and went into consultation with the Major Navigator. Ted and I ignored them and kept signing in. The AC finally came up next to me and looked me up one side, down the other, and went back to the up side. I ignored him. He finally coughed and asked, " Are you in the same Airforce that I'm in?" I decided to inspect him and did the upside and down side inspection in return. He just stood there and waited until I was finished. I waited a second or so and then said very loudly, " NO!"

He almost jumped back, stammered an "Excuse me", and shuffled back to his crew with the fat Navigator. Ted and I picked up our custom tailored Hang-up Bags and dragged them behind us as we really swaggered down the hall and turned the corner of the corridor. We then ran to our rooms laughing like idiots, praying that the Light Bird would stay confused.

I have listened to several different folk tell that story and, so far, none have gotten it right. Neely Johnson even had it published in a magazine and it was only close. Ted and I managed to get away with another close call and still laugh about the guys with the spoons in their pencil pockets. Do you still wonder why so many folk think that Fighter Pilots are arrogant?

CHAPTER TWENTY-THREE
CHAFF BOMBS

Since I had my hold baggage rifled when I left Takhli in Dec '67, I have only my very faulty memory to go on for this tale. I think this all happened in mid to late June '67 but I may be off by a couple of weeks.

My Bear, Carlo Lombardo, the grouchy one wanted to talk to me about Chaff. I knew zip about the stuff except that it messed with Radar and that it had been used during WWII and was then called Window. He introduced me to several EWO's who wanted to see if there was some way to deploy chaff by dropping a bomb or bomb-like thing filled with cut chaff. I had been to the Weapons School in '66 and had not even heard of chaff there.

We yammered for a while and decided that it might be possible to hand cut some chaff to the best length for the Radars of interest in NVN and put it in a SUU-30. A SUU is a Suspension and release Unit that can be filled with a BLU (Bomb Live Unit) and is then called a CBU or Cluster Bomb Unit. Everyone is overjoyed to invent a language. The SUU-30 was the can that held the Soft Ball sized BLU's that made up the CBU-24. The weight of that seemed adequate for their idea. I checked with Sam Adams and he agreed that it might work. Carlo had several EWO's from both the Weasels and the B-66's who were more than willing to work at the idea.

The first tasks were to cut the chaff by hand, load the stuff into a SUU-30, weigh it and get it balanced. This took about a week. I managed to get through to Sarah Renshaw at Eglin and talk her into stealing some computer time and sending Sam and me some ballistic charts. As usual Sarah did her normal good work and we got a pile of printout in a short time. In the interim the EWO's cut enough chaff for several bombs and made sure they were balanced. We were ready to go.

I talked Col Bob White into letting me drop one chaff bomb close to a GCI site to see what would happen. We picked Moonglow near NKP and he got permission for the test. I flew down in a Weasel 'F' with two chaff bombs loaded and they directed me where to drop. Those two bombs held about 500 pounds of chaff each and, when dropped, they created a thunderstorm sized return on Moonglow's scope that blocked over half the Blue Anchor Refueling tract for an hour. It worked!!

Col White agreed to try an attempt to create a chaff cloud in RP-6 between the end of Thud Ridge and Phuc Yen as soon as we were going back to that area. We got 12 chaff bombs ready and Sam and I came up with a plan of where and how. Not very long after that we were fragged to the area and Col White let us try our trick. He was the Force CC, Shark, and I was his Weasel, Barracuda. Bill Campfield, one of our very best Weasels leaders was flying number three; so, I assigned his element to drop the Chaff, while I chased SAM's. It is a wonder that Bill still talks to me and hasn't shot at me for that trick because it was a tiny bit hairy.

He was to take his element out into the flats headed a bit north of Phuc Yen, flying at a minimum of 600KCAS, pull up to about 15,000 and loft the chaff. Bill was welcomed by a large number of SAM's and a very large number of guns of all types. He did his job as instructed and created a huge monsoon type chaff cloud that blocked all the Radars that tried to look through it. The Bad Guys shot a bunch of Guideline Missiles at the cloud that made it a bunch bigger and probably rained several tons of scrap onto the Rice Paddies. Bill did tell me that in his opinion my parents were not legally wed and that he did not look with favor on me! The bottom line was that it worked and added another trick to our play book.

We were able to use the chaff bombs to very good use several times after that and it even got someone looking at dispensers for our birds. In addition we got several ideas of different ways to toss CBU-24's that had never been tried before that also added to our play book. I hope Bill isn't still of the opinion that Coy and Kathleen were not wed because it would make them sad.

CHAPTER TWENTY-FOUR
ONE WAY TO WEASEL:
CARLO & SPARKY'S WAY

When I went through the Weasel School in early '67 I didn't have the foggiest idea of what a Weasel did for a living other than they were supposed to hunt down and kill SA2 SAM sites. Chuck Horner and White Fang Hartney decided that it would be the funniest thing in the world to have Carlo Lombardo and me team up. The odds were 7 to 5 that we would kill each other in less than a week. So much for Officer Horner!

The best thing that could have happened was for me to have Carlo as my Bear. We did argue just a wee bit; however, neither of us ever really wanted to kill the other. Almost all Weasel EWO's got a nickname either at Nellis or in SEA. Carlo became Grouchy Bear for very good reason halfway through the course. The only EWO known only as 'Bear' or 'The Bear was Jerry Hoblit's own trained, performing Bear, Tom Wilson.

Carlo knew enough   about Fighter Types to

know that they needed to be taught at least the basics of Electronic Warfare. He started me off with the equivalent of EW 101 and I never got to the 200 course. I had been in the business for over eight years in USAFE and TAC and did not really know squat about the systems that were designed to kill me other than Aircraft. Carlo taught me about EW with all of the emphasis on SAMs and Gun-layers. By the time we left Nellis I at least knew that I didn't know squat and that Carlo sure as hell did!

We got to Takhli, 357TFS, and he really turned up the gain on the lessons. We flew our first mission on the wing in RP-6 and for the first time I heard all of that damned noise Carlo understood. We met all of the Radars on Day One and even saw two SAMs in flight. It was a very sobering trip and I did realize that I sure needed to listen and understand what my Bear was saying. My second Weasel sortie was in a "D" flying number 4 in a Weasel flight. I listened to the racket from the APR25-26 and the Shrike and even recognized some of the squeaks and squawks. Mission number three on day three was as Barracuda lead on the Dawn Patrol, a fairly quick check out for Carlo and me. We managed to get Shark in and out with no losses. Carlo and I then spent over 5 hours in Intell figuring out what we had done, just the two of us, walking the planning area and trying to decide how to do understand this god-awful mess. Carlo suggested that he build a picture of what the Radar Order of Battle looked like each time we went to the Barrel so we could use the best tactics for the situation.

I was about as uninformed about how the systems all played together as my dog and needed to really work on my ability to understand what was out there gunning for us. Carlo tried to teach me as quickly as he could. We would go down to the Operations center every time we were scheduled for a mission, either as lead or wing, and spend at least 2 to 3 hours looking at the maps and photos on the walls. We would study all of the latest intelligence we had and try to figure out how it was being orchestrated by the Hanoi Cowboys.

It was a ritual and we started to be able to retain more and more of what we were looking at. Carlo would start looking at Radar systems as soon as we dropped of the tanker each mission in an orderly way. He would look for BARLOCK, the big arrays that were used to track us and then send the MIGs in for intercepts. After he checked for BARLOCKS, he would look for Height-finder Radars since they were vital for direction of MIGs to the right altitude. He would start looking for Gun-layer Radars and count the number that were looking in our direction early since they could track the jamming noise from our pods. The more Gun-layers, the more attention we could expect when we got into the Hanoi Valley. He used all of our gear, the APR-25/26, the Shrike sounds, and his APR-142 and every possible mode. By the time we flew to the Black River, Carlo had a very good picture of how the Bad Boys were set up to shoot at us.

I flew 24 Combat sorties in June '67, our first

month. We were scheduled every day and were weather canceled 7 times. Of the 24 sorties we flew, we led 18 of the 24. We flew 18 in RP-6 and led 15 of those. We were very busy and very tired. Carlo had almost set a pattern in how we conducted each sortie. He would build his picture of what was waiting for us and would suggest just how many and how ferocious the SAMs would be. He was starting to be able to predict the MIG activity with more and more accuracy. I was starting to be able to catch what he was trying to tell me and I was getting so I could hold more and more in my head.

Carlo kept up his attempt to understand what was operating each day and changed his techniques as time went by to better understand what the Bad Guys were doing. He also never stopped trying to educate the Nose Gunner, AKA Sparky, on the finer points of EW. We had become a very smooth team. We had one extremely weird day when not one signal came up. Carlo was totally confused and bitched constantly.

We had 4 EWOs in the flight and all of them were nervous as long tailed cats in a room of rocking chairs. Our gear was working and nothing was being intercepted. We went into and out of the target with zero signals. Carlo and I were scared spitless and fretted like crazy. NO SIGNALS WILL SCARE YOU HALF TO DEATH! It only happened once and I still remember being really jumpy.

As we neared the Hanoi Valley when we were headed to RP-6, Carlo would start to drop the non-threat Radar commentary. This would normally happen as we crossed the Black River or about half way to the Northeast Rail Road. By then the big picture was built and I had a very good idea about whether it would be a MIG day or a SAM day or both. Very seldom did both MIGs and SAMs come up and threaten at the same time. I saw a SAII lift off and head away from the Weasels and the Force once as we passed by the middle of Thud Ridge. I checked way high at my left 8 and watched the missile smack an MIG-17 right in the wing root. Bad coordination by the Bad Guys but Good for us! Even Carlo could only talk so fast. The threats always take precedence over information systems. By late summer '67, we were like a very well oiled machine and could communicate with grunts and moans. I felt totally at ease with Carlo and trusted him to give me exactly what information I needed at the exact time. I'm sure that all of the good Weasel Crews have similar stories to tell about how we learned to really talk to each other.

Every Weasel crew had to be different since each crew was unique. I flew with a few other Bears after Carlo went to Saigon with Col White and we flat could not work the way Carlo and I did. I flew with all of the Instructor EWOs when I got back to Nellis and the same things occurred. I tried to work with Mike Gilroy who is as good as anyone and we were very different than Carlo and I had been. Unique abilities drive unique methods of coordination. The Weasel Mission required, and still requires, the very best coordination by the crew and between crews. If you can't communicate, you are in deep and serious crap. I was most fortunate to have Carlo to teach me how to stay alive and then give me the best possible information to do my job. Carlo used to bitch loudly that "All of the brains are in the back seat and all of the decisions are in the front seat"! He was right and that's the way it works best. The methodology of information transference doesn't matter as much as the ability to transfer information quickly and accurately. It ain't how you do it that matters as long as you do it right!

CHAPTER TWENTY-FIVE
BARLOCK RADAR

The Soviet supplied BARLOCK long range surveillance radars were used by North Vietnam to position MIG-21's for their best shot at the Force on the way in to North Vietnam, and to see our track in order to figure out each target. They only had two of the great big mothers in country and they were considered their Crown Jewels. The one that covered the west approaches was close to the Black River looking straight down our ingress routes. It could see us from the time we dropped off the Tankers in Laos until we left the country. It should have been THE prime target from the day it arrived. The second was situated north and a bit west of Haiphong looking out to sea and could cover the Navy attacks in to Haiphong and our water route ingress routes that came in over the Cam PHA Mines. It also should have been a prime target. Neither was ever on any target list. They were not *verboten*, just never targeted.

The BARLOCK was huge and had 6 transmitters all with a slightly different frequency. They were mounted in a very large array that rotated. Each Radar transmitter was set a slightly different elevation angle in order to give them a good idea of our altitude even without Height Finder Radars co-located. The transmitters were each about 6 Megawatt and damned near impossible to jam. They were very good and the North treasured them and put a large bag of guns around each one as well as covering them with excellent camouflage netting. They were almost invisible.

Carlo figured out how they used them and what they used them for. He spent a considerable amount of time figuring out what other Radars were operating at the same time. This gave him a good idea of what systems related to the defenses we had to face. If the BARLOCK wasn't up, we never saw a MIG-21 and seldom saw a -17. If the BARLOCK was up but no height finders were operating, the MIG -21 would not be there but the 17's would often be around the target area. If both a BARLOCK and height finders were grunting and squawking, Mr. MIG -21 was going to show almost every time. If only the BARLOCK was up and a bunch of Gun Layers were looking at us way beyond their normal distance, Mister SAM was going to be a problem. They would track our Jamming package with as many as 20/30 Gun layers and have our track down pat.

What still gives me a bad itch below my shorts was that we were never briefed about any of this by Intel. In fact none of this was ever a subject by any of our Intel sources. Carlo seemed to be the only one who ever made any connection. I know that's bull brown; however, nobody in the Intelligence ever mentioned it.

Carlo convinced me that he really had broken the code and could tell whether it would be a MIG Day or a SAM Day. He was right every call for nearly a month when I decided to spread the word to the Force and especially to Olds lead. Carlo had figured out that there would be no MIGs when we were still a long way from the Black and I transmitted "Shark Force, this will not be a MIG Day, heads up for SAMs only near the target. This is Barracuda."

There were no MIGs and when we got home I got a call from Col Olds on the RED phone "How IN Hell Did You Figure That Out!" I explained and he believed me. What bugged me was that there were people who were charged with for these connections and were looking at better data that we had and never called out anything. Carlo kept up his good work until he left with Col White for 7th and he was never wrong on calling 'MIG Day', or 'No MIG Day'. He was able to make this distinction well over half the time. This information allowed the MIG CAP and the Weasels to shift our tactics to match requirements before we were in the Barrel. It also allowed the Force Commander to put his attention on only the most probable threat and cut his workload a bunch.

It would have been nice if all of the Alpha Strikes could have had the information passed to them as they flew toward the Barrel. The resources were there and looking at the same raw data the Carlo had on his 2" CRT. It never happened.

CHAPTER TWENTY-SIX
BARLOCK KILL

Carlo found a Barlock located almost on a line between channel 97 and Yen Bai. We couldn't find the sucker since he would go off the air when we got within 10 miles or so. We looked for his specific location all of July and part of Aug '67. We were unable to complete a mission in PACK-6 one afternoon because of weather and decided to road RECCE the Black River for several miles checking out old sites that were prepared for SAMs/Guns. We did this ever so often to make sure that the bastards didn't sneak one in on us. I would fly over a section of the river valley and roads and then come back at about 600 KTS and 4,000' with an empty station selected. I'd press the bomb button to start the KB-70 Camera running and jink over the area of interest. The KB-70 was a 70mm camera with a rotating lens that took 4 frames per second with each frame covering a swath 8 degrees wide and almost 180 front to back. We would keep this up until we ran out of gas and/or film for the KB-70. The INTELL section would develop the film and a Photo Interpreter (P I) would check it for anything of interest. We were in debriefing and very sharp SSGT came out to get me. He said that he had a super set of shots that he had stereoed. Carlo and I went back with him and he had several super stereo shoots looking UP at a BARLOCK camoflaged under a huge set of nets located on a karst ridge on the north side of the Black River about in the middle of the area we had been checking.

I TOLD HIM TO HOLD EVERYTHING. I went to the debriefing area and dragged Col Bob White in to look at the shots. He was grinning like a teenager at a nudist convention. He told me that he would try and get us FRAGGED for the site. The next day we went back to PACK-6 and were weathered out again. He held the Force just short of the Red River and told me to join up. He then gave me the lead of the Force, 16 F-105D's, and told me to find the BARLOCK. He did this without asking anyone for forgiveness and ignored the Fragged backup target. That takes cajones of massive size!

I led back to the Black and put all four flights in a holding pattern. The lead Flight had two three thousand pound M-118s each fused with the old VT fuses. I rolled in and strafed the tops of the trees over the site to mark the area. Col White dropped both his three-grinders and they opened up the camouflage. Guns started shooting from all around the site from the valley floor and the karst ridge. I called each aircraft in that had m-118s singly and had each one hit guns. That fairly settled the guns down. I had 4 birds with CBU-24 and 8 with M-117 GP bombs (750 lb class) left and put them in one at a time. There were no SA-2s anywhere near and the guns were very little threat.

When we left we had put eight M118, 3,000lb bombs, 48 M117, 750lb bombs, 24 CBU-24 munitions from Shark Force and an additional 8 CBU-24 munitions and all my 20MM from Barracuda. The BARLOCK was not even a greasy spot on the karst ridge.

To end the day, Korat was also weathered out. Mike Muskat heard us, came over and checked what we were doing. He called in the Korat Force and they dropped all their ordnance as well. That was a very dead BARLOCK.

We had no MIG-21 activity for several weeks after that. I think that this lucky event should have cued someone that taking out the BARLOCKs would have been a good idea. We could have and we also could have KILLED all of their SAM equipment as well as we did in LINEBACKER if we had been allowed.

CHAPTER TWENTY-SEVEN
TACTICAL CONSIDERATIONS
LOMBARDO & SPARKS 1967

When Carlo and I got to Takhli in mid May '67,
we were dumber than dirt. The only thing good about
that was we knew our limitations. I had dental surgery
done two days after we arrived and was grounded for
2 weeks. By the time my mouth was cleared for
chewing, I had spent a ton of time talking to
whomever I could find that seemed to have their
Sierra in a sack. Hoblit and Wilson had spent all night
with us as soon as we arrived trying to transfer a tour
of information to the rookies. I was sure of two
things; I didn't know squat and that Carlo was more
knowledgeable about Electronic Warfare than anyone
on the base. To ameliorate the situation, I had flown
63 missions from Takhli in '65, was a Weapons
School Graduate, and had about 1200 hours in the
Thud. That's not a bad place to start building your
Tactical bag of Tricks.

We started our tour by flying on Bill Campfield's
wing the first day of June. I flew the next morning in a

'D' due to the shortage of 'F' models and found myself on the schedule to lead Barracuda Flight supporting Shark Force (Col. Bob White) the early morning go on 3 June. Carlo and I went to the Ops Center with Col. White to help plan the Mission.

We made it in and out of PACK-6 without losing anyone. After a long debrief, we immediately started to work on our very obvious shortcomings. We would spend at least one hour prior to each mission going over all of the annotated map and photo boards on the walls of the planning area. The reason for this was to pound into our heads where all of the threats were given the state of the intelligence we had. This allowed us to visualize the angles to the best guess prepared SA-2 sites from our planned area of responsibility. I worked at being able to spot definite points on the ground that would allow me to time a pull-up and Shrike launch at any of the SA-2 sites we expected to be operating. Carlo looked at the angular relationships of all of the expected sites in the area. We continued to do this as long as we flew there. All Tactics depend on the area and the Mission. The other unchanging fact is that Tactical planning also depends on who the hell is flying on each mission. Everyone is different and their strengths and weaknesses dictate what a flight can and cannot do intelligently.

Tactics are not magic tricks that will make the other side run away. They are only a set of more or less workable idea on what formations to fly, feints to use, directions of attack that allow you to best come back another day, and anything else that the Flight Leader can imagine that will give him an edge. One feint was to point at a radiating site, pull up for a Shrike launch, and then not launch. The SAM operator would usually pull the plug and go off the air for about one minute before coming back up. One of the best spin-offs of this Tactic was an idea that Phil Drew came up with. We were, as usual, having trouble getting hits with the Shrike because the SAM boss would shut down his Radar after he thought we had launched. Phil suggested that we pull up into a typical Shrike Launch, fake a shot, fly the rest of the maneuver, and pull out high and turn tail to the SAM still at altitude. This should convince the SAM operator that a real Pigeon was fluttering along not looking at him. The trailing Weasel could come in about 45seconds behind the initial shooter at low altitude.

After the first shooter did his act, the trailer could launch a low loft at the same site and expect the Radar to come back on and catch the Shrike. It sounded like a good idea and we briefed it far a mission not far from Hanoi. I was the faker and Phil was the sneaky shooter. It worked like a charm for three consecutive days. Phil's Shrike smacked the Radar just as he was shooting at me and blew the antennae away. We tried the same thing about every other mission for over a week before they wised up and stopped getting caught. My only problem with that Tactic was that I was the bait and someone else was the killer. Being bait means that even if you aren't eaten you get all soggy and don't look too good. Tactics are ephemeral and the best rule is to not repeat some cute trick too often or you will get caught.

Tactical formations always depend on both the experience of the crews and the type and intensity of the threat. If there are no MIGs, loose formations with the element split as much as 5 miles worked very well. If there were MIG-17's, the formation should stay closer and the splits should be less. If MIG-21's were in the area, a much closer formation was required. Airspeed in the Threat area was also a very big item. The more likelihood a MIG-21 would visit meant that the Airspeed should never go below 540 except during an attack or very hard turn. The number and type of guns in the area also dictated altitude, airspeed, and formations that were best. The number of SAM site that were active in the area were also drivers. Few SA-2s allowed greater splits and looser formations while more of the damned thing meant that we had to keep a bit closer for mutual coverage.

If this sounds like too many things to cover in a briefing, you are right. My briefings were more general in nature and almost always consisted of more general guidelines. Airspeed was my only absolute command. Thou Shall Never Commit The Sin Of Flying Slowly! 540 knots was my minimum when in Pack 6. It was stupid to give the MIGs a chance and fast was the answer. If airspeed was kept up, very little afterburner was ever required. I stayed in Pack 6B for 58 minutes with a flight of four and had fuel to make Danang when we left. Airspeed was life. The other unbreakable rule was altitude. To fly below 4,500' was a death wish. The only time anyone should fool around below that floor if it became mission essential. On a Rescue all rules were null and void if the pickup required it.

This maunder on Tactics has very few Tactics in it. The reason for this is that Tactics are always things of the moment and depend on far too many real time factors to be canned and slavishly followed after any briefing. I am convinced that any TACTIC that is written down should only be flown when some Stand-Eval Twerp is breathing down your neck and can do damage to your boss. If I can convince people of the very short life of any Tactic, I'll be happy. Tricks are another kettle of fish

All Flight Leaders must have a Bag of Tricks available to use in flight. The melding of this array of maneuvers, formations, airspeeds, Etc are the stock-in-trade for any decent Fighter Pilot. The ability to reach into his bag and produce the appropriate set of tricks is what makes a good Flight Lead. The best Weasels were the ones who looked like Harry Houdini as they made the selected old maneuvers look new and shiny.

I think I have maundered enough about specific that were germane 40 years ago. The only good that could come from this drivel would be to have some folk think about the Threat, their own capabilities, and plan a way to best defeat the threat.

CHAPTER TWENTY-EIGHT
CARLO'S BEST DAY

Carlo Lombardo, Grouchy Bear, was my Electronic Weapons Officer (EWO) for my second tour. The method of selecting designated crews at the Wild Weasel School was a bit strange. We had to select each other, jump over a broom, and then be 'Married' for 100 missions or death do you part. I had never met an EWO before and, all of a sudden, I am 'Married' to this big, old, grouchy person for my second combat tour at Takhli. We didn't kill each other during training, graduated, and arrived at Takhli RTAFB, Thailand in May '67. All EWOs were affectionately known as Bears, all Bears had nicknames, and Carlo was dubbed 'Grouchy Bear'. The name was fitting.

Carlo and I flew a bunch of excellent missions and managed to rack-up five photo confirmed SAM kills complete with secondary fires and explosions. I am convinced that Carlo's very best mission was flown in August 1967 when Carlo and I were scheduled to lead the Weasel Flight, Barracuda, on a mission to Hanoi.

The assignment to lead Alpha Strikes rotated through the three squadrons of the 355th Tactical Fighter Wing (355TFW) at Takhli Thailand. On this Mission, Colonel Bob White, Wing Director of Operations (355TFW/DO), was the Force Commander for Shark Force. We had the normal Alpha Strike (Hanoi Package) setup consisting of two flights from the 357th Squadron (357TFS), my Squadron, and one each from the 333rd and 354th. The MIGCAP was from the 8th Wing at Ubon. The Target for this mission was downtown Hanoi near the center of the city. The F-105Ds were all configured with two 450-gallon fuel tanks on the inboard stations, a Jamming Pod outboard and a Multiple-Ejector-Rack (MER) centerline. The MER allowed us to carry up to six weapons on each rack, Shark was carrying six CBU-24 Cluster Bombs for flak suppression and the other three strike flights had six M117 750-pound bombs.

The four F-105F Weasels had our standard configuration consisting of a single CBU-24 on each inboard pylon, a Shrike Anti-Radiation-Missile (ARM) on each outboard station, and a 650-gallon centerline tank. That load was best for us since it allowed us to kill Surface-To-Air-Missile Sites (SAMs), keep our MACH up, and have the endurance to stay in Route Package Six (RP-6) for at least thirty minutes. The four-ship MIGCAP flight of F-4D aircraft had a standard load of Heat Seeking AIM-9 and Radar directed AIM-7 missiles,   Jammers, and fuel tanks.

Since we were the early morning launch, we planned the mission the afternoon before with Col White and a few guys from the 357TFS. SAM activity had been very low for a couple of weeks and I hadn't seen a Guideline Missile in the air for over two weeks. When the SAM activity dropped off like that, the situation normally shifted to a sharp increase in Missile firings a few days later. The bad guys operating the SAMs would get scared after we killed a site or two and they would pull in their horns. Their bosses would get on their cases and the SAM drivers would come out shooting for a while. We would smack them another serious lick and the cycle would repeat. Carlo and I had decided that this day might be a busy one and we had better be ready to dodge at a great rate if it looked like it would be a "SAM Day". We discussed this with Colonel White and came up with a good plan for a SAM DAY.

We had three very good, very experienced crews scheduled to fly with us. Barracuda Lead and Two were from the 357TFS, the element lead, Three, from the 354th, and Four from the 333rd. Each Pilot was Weasel flight lead qualified, the low time jock had over 2000 hours of fighter time, all four EWOs were aggressive, and everyone had been to RP-6 more than they wanted to. All four crews had flown together as a flight several times before and we expected a smooth, very disciplined flight. Disciplined it was, however, it was to be very rough rather than smooth.

Shark Force, all twenty crews plus spares, briefed at 0-dark-30, did the usual individual flight briefings, normal pre-flight stuff, and the whole Gorilla taxied on time for a pre-dawn takeoff in the very black Thai night. Everything was a piece of cake through the refueling on Green Anchor in northern Laos. After the entire Force refueled, I moved the Weasels out to about ten minutes in front of Shark Force.

Carlo was doing his standard bit of trying to figure out the Radar Order Of Battle for the day. He would start while we were still in Northern Laos and use every piece of gear in the aircraft. Carlo's office was my back seat. The instrument panel had been modified and two extra systems installed. The first was the ER-142 System designed to listen to all of the electronic signals the band width used by the Gun Director Radars and the SAM Radars in North Vietnam. It had a very small scope, a little over 2", and controls that allowed him to select a signal, shift to a time based scan, and determine what the radar was doing. The system was clumsy and hard to use; however, it allowed us to find and kill the threats.

The second set of gear was the APR-35/36 Radar Homing and Warning (RHAW) system. The RHAW system consisted of a round scope that visually and aurally showed the type, direction, and approximate range to a set of threats and a billboard showing the threats received. One of the lights on the display in both seats was the Launch Light. The Launch Light indicated that a Missile guidance signal was being transmitted. In addition to the light there was a loud tone transmitted. Carlo could listen to the Launch Tone and tell if the guidance triplets were moving or not. If they were, it was guiding a missile, if not it was a false signal. If any of you remember "Disregard the Launch Light, it not valid!" That was one way Carlo could distinguish a Valid from an Invalid signal.

The RHAW gear was in both cockpits. In addition to the ER-142 and the RHAW gear, we could listen to the signals picked up by the Shrikes. Carlo would have me turn up the audio on the Shrike Missile and slowly move the nose around to see what he could hear in that spectrum. He would have the Shrike audio turned back down and would use the ER-142 in all of its' modes, creating all sorts of strange squeaks and squawks. He'd diddle with the APR35/36 by pressing the Press-To-Test buttons. That defeated the logic of the system and allowed him to get a raw feed from each band. All of these strange noises made little sense to me; however, they made a bunch of sense to Carlo. He was especially interested in the fairly high-pitched EEK/EEK made by height finder Radars and the much lower pitched, more slowly spaced UNKs from the BARLOCK (GCI) Radars. When a Radar beam passed across our aircraft, we could hear the Pulse Recurrence Frequency (PRF) that was unique to that Radar. This produced the squeaks and squawks.

If there were no GCI Radars operating and only one or two height finders, we could expect very little trouble from the MIGs. We never saw an MIG-21 without a BARLOCK and two or more height finders up and operating. If we could expect few MIGs, our problem was easier.

Carlo then started checking out the number of FIRECAN Gun Layer Radars that were up. They gave out the normal modulated sizzling sound that always seemed to be in the background. Carlo had figured out a month or so back that since they could not see us at ranges of 75 miles or greater, they were being used to track the blob of jamming put out by the 16 ship Strike force and the trailing MIGCAP. Although the Radars were denied range, by using several FIRECANs they could get line-of-sight bearings to the jamming blob and they could then triangulate our position and track our course.

The ideas seemed logical. According to Carlo I was only a nose gunner and not very bright. He would tell me what was really happening and I was to shut up and listen. I seldom argued with Grouchy Bear and never won. There were three reasons: First, he was older than God, second, he was downright irate when crossed, and third, he was always right. Carlo had joined the US Army two weeks before I entered the First Grade in '41. He was in one of the first classes for Electronic Warfare (Old Crows) in '42. He had more electronic warfare experience than anyone I ever met and was an exceptional EWO indeed. I was extremely fortunate to have him in my 'Pit. Carlo was 49 and earned his nickname, Grouchy Bear.

On this day we had more FIRECANs than anyone in the flight had ever seen as we crossed into NVN from Laos. They were all operating from well inside North Vietnam and watching our track inbound to the Red River. The FIRECAN activity coupled with GCI Radar and no height finder transmissions meant that we should expect few enemy fighters. It was looking like a SAM day.

As we headed for the Red River crossing point, the count of FIRECANs increased until the ER-142 scope was almost solid in that bandwidth. Carlo estimated over thirty gun-layers up at one time. We started to pick up the rattlesnake noise of a couple of SAM Radars along with the associated blinking strobes on the Radar Warning Scope as we passed the Black River, well short of the Red River, and the count started up. This was earlier than normal for the Vietnamese SAMs. In fact, all Radar activity was much higher than we were used to. Carlo had been right. It was shaping up as a real SAM DAY.

By the time we crossed the Red River and turned towards Thud Ridge, a range of 3000 to 5000 foot mountains northwest of Hanoi, we had more SA-2 Radars up that I had ever encountered. Carlo counted a total of eighteen different SAM Radars by the time we were about to enter the outer Hanoi ring of missiles. Our best Intelligence estimate was that they only had 21 in the whole country. Carlo always kept a steady stream of commentary going that covered all of the threats we were about to meet and as much additional information that he thought I could handle. He could hit peaks of 10,000 words a minute on a good day. As we passed the middle of the ridge, maybe thirty miles out from the valley, he told me he was dropping all guns because he couldn't break them out and would only call 3-Ring SAMs. This meant that

I was to look out for the more than 10,000 guns in the valley since he was too busy with the SAMs to help, very reassuring. I had never heard him do that before and figured that we were in deep trouble and hadn't even gotten into the Hanoi area yet.

For those of you who haven't been there, the Hanoi area is about the size of the Las Vegas Valley. Thud Ridge (named because of the number F-105s buried there) runs from the Northwest toward Hanoi. We preferred to come down the ridge towards the city since there were no guns on the ridge, it was easy to see, and it gave us a place to play hide and seek with the Radars in the flats. The valley floor was as level as a pool table, has no place to hide, and extends all the way to the Gulf Of Tonkin south of Haiphong. What we had were eighteen SA-2 sites in an area about thirty miles in diameter. For the next 28 minutes we faced no fewer that sixteen at any one time, all operating simultaneously, and all in-range for a shot. We were headed for a very busy day.

One of the reasons that Carlo was a Grouchy Bear was his working environment. I would turn off the aircraft pressurization system (This included the air-conditioner) in case we took a hit and caught fire. The cockpit temperature would rapidly hit 120. If you intended to stay alive in RP-6, you had to 'Jink' randomly in order to keep the aimed Flak from hitting you. That translates randomly jerking the bird up, down, right, or left at 3 to 4 seconds intervals. Carlo had to keep his head buried in the cockpit peering at the scopes and fiddling with the controls. While he was leaning over trying to make sense from chaos, the idiot in the front continually jinked around like a frog on a stove. It would make a buzzard puke. He never missed a beat, never put Caesar Salad on his scopes, or even bitched. All he did was groan when I hit 7 'G'. He had every right to be a Grouchy Bear.

I split Barracuda Flight into our normal formation of two cooperating elements in a staggered trail about three miles apart. Every time either element would head for a site to take it down, it would stay up and three or more others would challenge us. Normally, when you headed directly towards a SAM site, it would drop off the air and another would come up and try to catch you from a blind spot. Not this day, they came up, stayed up, and kept shooting missiles. The APR-35 scope had three concentric rings etched on it from the center dot to the case. Any signal strobe that extended from the center to 2 ½ rings or more was considered to valid threat and in range to fire a missile with a good chance of a kill. A "Four-Ringer" (out to the edge of the case) was really close, heart of the envelope shot, and a "Waterfall" (bouncing off the case) was cause for browning of the shorts. Needless to say, we had almost continuous "Four-Ringers" and numerous "Waterfalls" for what seemed forever. The scope seemed to be full of blinking SA-2 threats with most of them extending to the case.

A phenomenon of stress is that time becomes elastic and seconds seem like minutes or, in other words, time flies when you're having fun. I never, before or after, saw so many SAM Radars up or so many SA-2 missiles in the air. We came up with a count of approximately 72 launches during the debriefing. I really don't know how many there were. I do know that Carlo called every launch to include the bearing and approximate distance. He called them by saying they were targeted at Barracuda (lead element), Barracuda Three (the element), or the Force. I had to dance with 12 separate firings that day alone.

When a SAM is being directed at you, you dance with it. First you visually acquire the missile in flight, turn to place it at your right 2-O'clock or left 10-O'clock, push up the power, lower your nose for extra airspeed, and wait until it is about to hit you. While you are watching the supersonic telephone pole approach, you alternately pull up and then push down in order to see if it is tracking. If it is tracking, it apparently sags or rises and then settles back to a tracking position.

When you think it is about to hit you and can't stand it any longer, you pull up and into the missile with at a minimum of 4"G", which normally overshoots to at least 7. This will cause the missile to miss, break apart, or go ballistic. The Guideline Missile can pull 25 'G', however, the rolling pull up causes it to require at least 35 and it can't hack the turn. You have just been forced to dance with a very ugly partner. Barracuda Element had about the same number to jig with as lead. I would line up a site and try to fire, or have my wingman fire, a Shrike. If we were lucky, we could get the Shrike off before we had to waltz with another incoming flying telephone pole smoking along at almost MACH Three.

At sometime during the fray, I had the flight jettison the 650-gallon centerline tanks to give us a bit more maneuverability and staying power since we were really going through the gas. After about 15 minutes of this extreme amount of fun, my element was forced to join up with me. The element lead had to do this because his EWO, and his wingman's EWO, had both lost the electronic picture of the fight and all four heads were now out of the cockpits looking for supersonic telephone poles. My wingman's EWO also had to go head out for the same reason. This left Carlo as the only EWO with his head down, watching the scopes, deciding what all eighteen SAM sites were doing, and calling the shots for Barracuda flight. We basically were just rolling with the punches and absorbing missiles to cover the Strike Force.

Shark came down Thud Ridge, located the target, and hit it while a hail of missiles was being fired at the Weasels. Less than half the missiles headed anywhere close to the position of the strike force. Of those that were fired at toward Shark Force, all were wide misses. Shark made it to the target and through rejoin without having anyone hit, or having to really dodge a single missile. During all this time, Barracuda Flight spent over 26 consecutive minutes inside the overlapping missile envelopes of sixteen or more SAM sites. Carlo called every shot and kept up a running commentary on 'What's Happening'. If he had hiccupped, even once, we would have been history. The bad folk were after the Weasels for sure and pulled out all the stops to get us. They failed. My shorts were very brown and, I suspect the rest of Barracuda flight had the same problem. We all made it.

We still had our CBU-24's as we finally followed Shark and the MIGCAP out of the valley because we just flat couldn't pick out a site and hit it due to the activity all around us. I would have lost at least one or more wingmen had I tried. We found a 57mm gun site near Thud Ridge and killed it with our CBUs on egress. I didn't have the foggiest idea whether we hit any radar emitters with our Shrikes. We were a bit too busy to really determine if we hit anyone or not. We tried to determine what, if anything, we hit during debriefing and decided we hit an emitter with more than four and less than all eight of our Shrike shots. I still don't care. We did as well as we could.

Shortly after we crossed the Red River, Carlo called "Cold Mike" (no transmissions) and went dead silent. He stayed cold mike until I turned on initial at Takhli almost an hour later (His first transmission as we turned for the break was "Check your *******
lanyard"). I could smell the cigarette smoke all the way to Takhli (450+ miles) while he decompressed. I checked our fuel and decided that we did not need any gas from our post strike tanker and went directly home at over 30,000 and landed ahead of Shark

Force. I think all of us were too beat to really care.

As usual after an interesting mission, I got the whips and jangles as I wound down. We were way too busy to be nervous while we were in the barrel. Going home was as good a time to calm down, decide what happened, and how to do better next time. I decided that we had done about as well as we could and that Carlo was the key to what we did right. To this day, I have never seen anyone function as well, or even nearly as well as he did that day. Grouchy Bear was the very best, at least that day. There is an Oriental curse "May you be born in interesting times". The curse was obviously aimed at Barracuda. The only person who knew how truly afraid I became was my laundress and I slipped her enough extra coin to keep her silent.

We had a very lengthily debriefing with INTEL. Carlo conducted most of it. Grouchy Bear was never at his best in debriefings and had a habit of really jumping down the necks of the young INTELL debriefers. We had all four tapes from the flight voice recorders to pull times and other information. He did a masterful job of recreating the mission, including which site shot which missile and from where. Colonel White came by our table and listened for a while and tapped me on the shoulder for a chat. I walked away with him and he said that this had been a very good mission. I replied that it was a Dog - Squeeze mission from our viewpoint. He smiled and reminded me that we were supposed to be 'First In and Last Out' and to 'Protect the Force'. He said that

that was what he had seen and to shut up. I normally agree with Colonels, especially those I like and respect. Colonel Bob White had and has all my respect. He asked if Carlo had a good day. I assured him that Carlo did everything except give milk. He suggested that he should get an award. I agreed and he recommended a Silver Star. I agreed and he asked "What about the nose gunner?" I told him that I had earned at most a tenth of an Air Medal (an Air Medal for every ten missions in RP-6 was standard). His reply was "Sounds about right to me". Carlo later received a Silver Star to go along with two others, and I got another tenth of an Air Medal. It still seems about right to me. Given the circumstances that day, I am convinced that we did about as well as we possible could to protect the Force.

Charles A. Lombardo was the bravest man I ever met. At the risk of having Bear Wilson, Mike Gilroy, and/or several other EWOs call me collect at 0200 some weekend for a sense of humor check, he was also the best EWO ever. He kept me alive on 49 trips downtown Hanoi, the majority as the lead Weasel. That alone makes him damned excellent. It is an honor to have been a part of an effort that demanded total dedication and competence. The Wild Weasel Mission saved a bunch of lives and was worth every bit of effort expended. To watch anyone perform at such an extreme level of excellence day after day was worth the heightened pulse rate and the subsequent whips and jangles. Carlo's day-to-day performance was uniformly outstanding and he never had a bad day. The Grouchy Bear just flat didn't make mistakes. Carlo, I want to thank you for making us a hell of a team. I also thank your family for lending you to me for that tour. You did a very hell of a job of keeping Kathleen Sparks' only child alive.

CHAPTER TWENTY-NINE
A VERY LONG DAY IN PACK SIX

North Vietnam was broken down into segments numbered from south to north. Pack Six was the most northern of the segments, contained Hanoi, and was by far the most heavily defended. Missions flown in Pack Six, or RP-6, were very difficult but easy to remember. On this particular mission nothing much happened exciting; however, it was unique since everything was off the cuff and really unplanned.

This was in early August 1967 and we flew one of the truly Dog-Squeeze water routes, Brown Anchor. Refueling tracks were named for a color. Every one hated the over water tracks due to the length of the mission, nearly six hours. The two over water refueling areas ran north along the Gulf of Tonkin and were parallel, Brown and Tan. Both ran from just north of the DMZ to a drop off point north of Than Hoa. Brown was closer to the coast of North Vietnam. For some reason we only seemed to be assigned those Anchors for afternoon missions so the

North Vietnamese gunners didn't have to squint into the sun. We would fly from Takhli about due east to coast out just near Hue and then northeast to the Brown track. We would refuel up track, drop off, and head north of Haiphong along the coast well out from land. We would turn toward the coast just north of the Kam PHA mines and head west to the targets. The ingress routes then normally went from the coast into the Northeast Railroad, Kep Airfield, BAC Giang, or some other choice area. The Return-To-Base (RTB) was the reverse. A round trip was almost 6 hours.

The mission for this day was a small bridge that was west of Bac Giang and, as usual, it was surrounded by guns and covered by about four or five SAM sites. Our Force Commander was Colonel Bob White with the call sign, Shark Lead. Colonel White was the Director of Operations (DO) for the 355TFW. The Mission consisted of a Strike package, Wild Weasels to protect the force from SAMs and a MIG CAP (Combat-Air-Patrol) to take care of the enemy fighters. The Strike Force had 16 F-105D aircraft with six bombs each, two 450-gallon fuel tanks, and Jamming Pods. The strike Force call signs were Shark, Marlin, Bear, and Wolf. Barracuda (four F-105F Wild Weasels) carried two AGM-45 Shrike Anti Radiation Missiles (ARM), two CBU-24 bombs, and a 650-gallon centerline tank each. The MIG CAP, Olds, from the 8th Wing consisted of four F-4Ds with AIM-9, AIM-7 missiles, fuel tanks, and Jammers. The 8TFW at Ubon had call signs that were cars. Strangely enough, Colonel Robin Olds always seemed to have 'Olds' as his call sign. Korat was 20 minutes ahead of us with a target within 10 miles or so of our area. They also consisted of 16 F-105D, four F-105F Wild Weasels, and a 4 ship MIG CAP also from Ubon.

Carlo Lombardo, my Electronic-Warfare-Officer (EWO), and I were doing our usual routine grousing about long, over water, rear end numbing 6-hour missions. As we approached Ubon, I heard a call on Guard that said " Sparky-Sparky come up 1234." This was repeated 3 or 4 times and I asked Carlo who had the call sign 'Sparky' when I heard " Damn It Sparky, I can't remember your call sign, come up 1234." I switched to his frequency and checked in. Major Baldwin was the Korat Force Commander and had a problem. All of his Weasels had aborted and he flat did not want to head in north of Haiphong with no Weasels. He wanted to know if I would cover them for their mission. I told him that I was only a Captain and I had better get my boss, Shark Lead, on frequency.

I went back and brought Shark Lead up. Colonel White and Baldwin discussed WTFO. I told both that it wasn't a very hard thing to do and Barracuda could cut it easy. White was worried about MIGs and said he would approve if Barracuda could have Korat's MIG Cap cover him instead of Ozark, the Korat Strike Force. Baldy's answer was " Hell, if you send them, they can have my wife, I want some Weasels!" It was agreed that I could cover both Korat and Takhli.

I changed Radio Channels, briefed Barracuda for about 30 seconds on the changes, and then switched the flight to Korat's Strike Freq. We cut about 45 degrees left of the heading to Danang in order to join up with Ozark Force off the coast of North Vietnam. We went between Vihn and Than Hoa to where I thought the Korat force would be, coasted out, and the whole string of tankers was smack in front of us. I joined with the lead low KC-135 (normal position for the Weasel Tanker) and filled up. We hit the drop point on time and headed for the mines.

I took Barracuda in about 20 miles or so in front with the Korat MIGCAP five miles behind us. This allowed us to root around for the SAMs and keep the Strike Force covered. We only had a few sporadic SAM signals along with the normal bunch of Firecan gun layers. I briefed my flight to drop the 650-gallon centerline tank as soon as it went dry to allow as much time as possible in the Pack. Sam Adams was Barracuda Three for the mission and was about as good as anyone I ever met. Both of our wingmen were almost as experienced.

We did our usual five-mile or so split into pairs in semi-trail and had some SAMs come up fairly seriously near the target. Sam covered me and I lined the SAM up for my wingman to take a Shrike loft shot. I covered Sam as he lined up on another SAM and had his wingman shoot an AGM-45 Shrike at it. The SAMs both went down and Korat hit the target bang on. We fell in trail with the Korat package and came out behind them with few problems except for another nosy SAM that we smacked with 2 Shrikes on the way out. Barracuda now had 1 Shrike each and our CBU-24s.

As we hit the coast, I picked up Shark Force about 10 miles out and pulled a hard 180 turn to stay in front of them. I went to Takhli Strike Freq. and checked in with Shark. We accelerated to 600 Knots to get 15 miles in front and led Shark back in to the target area using similar tactics as the first trip. Two more SAMs came up and we knocked them down with shrikes. Shark had nothing but guns around their bridge and put it into the water. We headed out behind Shark and Olds and hit a 57mm gun emplacement near the Northeast Railroad on the way out. We couldn't use the CBU-24 bombs on SAMs since they would not stay up and play long enough to find them.

As we neared the coast the second time, Colonel Robin Olds, Olds Lead, asked if we could cover them for another swing back through the area due to some MIG calls from the Radar Picket ship, Red Crown. At that time Sam Adams and I had one Shrike each, no bombs or centerline tank, while both wingmen had no ordnance except the gun. I waggled my wings and hand signaled Sam for a fuel check. He had enough for about 10 or 15 minutes more before we really had to scoot. I had a couple hundred pounds less. I told Olds we could cover him and sent Barracuda 2 and 4 to the tanker to RTB with the force.

Sam and I went back to the Northeast Railroad in

front of Olds. The F-4s worked the area until Olds 2 called Bingo (low fuel). We covered Olds at his six as they went out. When we hit the coast Sam and I had been in RP-6 for 58 consecutive minutes, had never gotten below 540 knots, and still had enough fuel remaining to make Danang straight in with 600 pounds of fuel (six to eight minutes flying time) a Piece Of Cake.

At this point I screwed the pooch. I was sightseeing and allowed Olds to get to the Tanker first (Very dumb thing to do when you are skoshi for petrol). No problem, Sam had 10 minutes fuel to play with and I had a bit less. Olds 2 was a brand new 1st Lieutenant on his very first Pack 6 mission. He forgot how to refuel and was really rocking and rolling behind the KC-135 filling station. It did not help to have both Robin Olds and Bill Kirk give him flying lessons while he made a fool of himself. Sam and I were starting to sweat a bit and Carlo began to gripe at me and state his belief that my parents had not been legally wed and other less charming comments. The poor LT kept making a fool of himself in front of his Wing King and one of the best fighter pilots in the world, Bill Kirk. After a subjectively long time, I called Olds and the following conversation ensued.

"Olds, Cuda, we are hurting"

"Barracuda, Bad?"

"Tres Bad Boss"

"Olds Two, get off the boom"

"Lead, I'm Bingo"

"Olds Two, get off the damned boom now!"

"Olds Two is bingo minus 500!"

"I don't care if you F****** die! Get off the boom NOW!"

Olds Two moved off and I had Sam refuel first with me very close on his wing. He had fuel to go straight in to Danang and still have 300 pounds (three minutes) and I had 100 less. Sam took about 3500 pounds and I did the same. We departed the tanker just north of Vihn and took a straight line for Takhli.

As we started our turn to RTB, I thanked Robin for the gas. He said "No sweat, Barracuda, thanks for the cover. OK Two, lets see you make a fool of yourself one more time!" Sam and I changed channels and headed for home.

Sam and I joined our flight at the INTEL debriefing and then had a separate debrief with Colonel White. Everyone was happy and we wrote it all up in the Tactics Book in case we had to do it again. At least I never had to do that again and I'm not sure anyone else did either.

As a footnote, as I was leaving the Wing Headquarters for the bar, I was told I had a call on the RED PHONE in the command center. It was Colonel Olds calling from Ubon to say Hello. He talked about the mission a bit and never asked how low on fuel we were. As he ended his chat, I asked if his Nugget ever got any gas. " The damned fool finally took fuel. Don't worry about that ass, he's going on the night mission and will never fly with me again!" I asked him a couple of years ago when we were skiing at Steamboat Springs if he remembered that mission and he told me "Hell yes. That jerk never did fly with me again."

I finished with over 100 missions in RP-6 and 58 consecutive minutes remains my max for time in an aircraft inside the Pack. I later had about 2½ consecutive hours in Pack 6, but that was on the ground waiting for a helicopter.

CHAPTER THIRTY
HELICOPTERS AT HOA LOC

In late Sept or very early October '67, Takhli was given a pop-up mission to Strafe Helicopters near Hoa Loc Airfield in Route Pack Six (RP-6). We had prepared to attack a Railroad Marshalling yard at Phu Tho about 25 miles Northwest of Hanoi. It was considered a fairly easy target since it was outside the main Hanoi coverage of SAM sites. Col. Bob White, 355TFW/DO, was the Force Commander of a 16 ship F-105-D bombers, 4 F-105-F Wild Weasels, and 4 F-4-D MIGCAP from Ubon (8TFW). I was leading the Wild Weasels as Barracuda Lead, George Guss (357TFS) was #2, #3, Bill Walen, was from the 333TFS, and #4, Davis, was from the 354TFS. It was not at all unusual for us to fly with people from all three squadrons in the Weasel Flight. The Force consisted of two flights of 4 from the 357TFS, Bob White leading Shark and Tommy Kirk Leading Marlin, one from the 354TFS, Dale Leatham leading Bear, and one flight from the 333TFS. This was

218

normal for all RP-6 missions. The Force Commander and the 2nd Flight were from the same squadron, and one each from the other squadrons.

We had just started the Mission Briefing in the Operations Center when we were told to scrub everything and plan to hit two targets, two flights to Phu Tho and two flights to Strafe (guns only for ordnance) 6 helicopters parked near Hoa Loc Airfield. Everyone went bonkers! We left the briefing room and went to planning and started to try and work up a plan to do something we had never seen before. Since Phu Tho was not covered as heavily as Hoa Loc and that it would take several passes to kill 6 helicopters with the gun, Hoa Loc got priority. The 8th wing also had a mission to try a new gimmick at Hoa Loc, level Radar Bomb the airfield. Bob White decided that he would lead the Strafe mission and Dale Leatham, Bear Lead, would take the 333TFS flight and hit Phu Tho. I told both of them that there was ZERO way I could cover both strikes since they were simultaneous and over 60 miles apart. In addition, Barracuda had been tasked to cover the 8TFW Strike at Hoa Loc that was to be 15 minutes later than the Phu Tho Strike. The fix was to have Dale go with no Weasel coverage, call Ubon and see if they could move up 10 minutes, and keep Barracuda in the Hoa Loc area to cover both the helicopters and the level bomb drop. We went back into the Briefing room with all of the folk and briefed the new tasking. I am sure that everyone in the room was convinced that this was the stupidest idea in the last six months. Strafing any thing in RP-6 was about as stupid an idea as possible. We were all sure that we would lose at least one and probably more at Hoa Loc. Strafing was only used in RP-6 when absolutely necessary during a Rescue or some other emergency.

While we were all in planning, the Flight Line people were busting their butts downloading bombs from 10 Thuds (8 primaries and 2 spares). Shark Flight had all been configured with 2 M-118, 3000#, bombs and a 650-tank centerline. Marlin had two 450 tanks on the wings and 6 M-117, 750# bombs centerline. The Cannon Cockers solved the problem by dropping the centerline MER racks with the bombs on them or dropping the full 650 tank full of gas. That was way above the limit for the bomb loader, but it worked and the birds were all reconfigured in less than 45 minutes total. We had the best maintenance in the world and easily the most motivated men in the universe.

We made our takeoff times, took gas from the tankers, dropped off in North Laos, and headed for the Black river. The MIGCAP joined up about 3 miles at 6 as briefed and I took Barracuda out 10 minutes ahead of the force to check out the area for SAM activity. We had the normal number of Firecan and SAM Radars up and sniffing plus three Height Finders and one BARLOCK, GCI Radar. The presence of the BARLOCK meant that we could expect MIG activity. I took a long poke past the Black toward the Red river and then accelerated straight at Hoa Loc. There was little SAM activity and only the normal amount of Gun Radars in the area. Shark came into the area and his number three, I think spotted a MI-8 under some netting about 4 miles northwest of the Airfield and called it out. A SAM came up about than and I took him down with a Shrike from Barracuda two. Both Shark and Marlin started a left hand square pattern just like a training range in Kansas. They found all of the Choppers by the second pass and were hitting them in turn. They were in 4 or 5 separate places in a fairly small area, all under netting.

On about the 3rd or 4th pass, a MIG-17 rolled in behind Marlin 4 and started to fire at him. I hollered for Marlin 4 to break with no action. I yelled his name and told him to break with no action. I had rolled in and hit the burner to catch the MIG and finally opened fire early to try and get him to break off his attack on Marlin 4. When I fired, the MIG went into a Zone-4 defense (standard Soviet defensive move) and then did a split 'S' from about 3,000'. I was closing at about the MACH and pulled high for a re-attack when George Guss decided to follow him through the split 'S'. George pulled over 7 'G' and blew dirt almost the length of the runway at Hoa Loc with a ton of guns shooting at him. The MIG headed for Hanoi. Two MIG-21s came by at about 10,000' and were attacked by our MIGCAP and they headed for home. Barracuda 2 and 4 both called Bingo and I sent them home. Barracuda 3 stayed with me. By now all of the helicopters had been hit and were burning, so, Shark called for a Bug-Out southwest. As he started his last pass, a SAM fired a single SA-2 at the force. I was in position to loft two Shrikes at him and then turned to put the missile at my six and went low to check the helicopters. I smoked by them at well over 600KTS and saw numerous fires and a couple of really bent rotors. As we left the area we had about enough gas to make Udorn with about 750 lbs.

On the way in, Barracuda 2 saw Firecan Radar on a small hill overlooking the area and asked permission to gun him. I told him to smack it and Gus rolled him off the road. On the way out, we hit the wreckage again and dropped our CBU canisters on a gun that was shooting at us. Post-strike refueling went smoothly and we all made it home. Shark and Marlin killed all of the Helicopters, Bear hit Phu Tho with no problems, and the 8th wing troops dropped the Radar bombs on Hoa Loc Airfield with no losses. Over all, it was a very good mission for all of us.

In 1974 at Kunsan Korea I met an Ex-Beret who told me why we were restricted to guns only; however, that's another story that may not be declassified yet.

CHAPTER THIRTY-ONE
MY LAST COMBAT MISSION
MOVEMBER 5, 1967

I flew my 145th and last combat mission 5 Nov '67, not by choice. I had arrived at Takhli Royal Thai Air force Base on March 15, 1967 after completing the Wild Weasel School at Nellis. I talked to my boss, Lt. Col. Obie Dugan, who was commander of the 357th Tactical fighter Squadron and our deal was that I would fly 100 missions as a Wild Weasel and then complete another 37 missions as a strike pilot. This would make me one of the first guys to get 200 missions in North Vietnam in an F-105, since I had flown 63 missions in '65 when the 563TFS had been at Takhli for 4 months. In fact it would make me one of the first to get 200 in anything, since Carl Richter at Korat would be the first to finish 200 in September.

My Boss sent me up the command chain. The Deputy for Operations for the 355th Tactical Fighter Wing (355TFW/DO), Colonel Bob White agreed as well. My next stop was with the Wing King of the 355TFW, Colonel Bob Scott, Colonel Scott also agreed and I was off to   the races.

By late October'67 I had flown 77 missions as a Wild Weasel and Carlo Lombardo and I become a hell of a fine Weasel Crew. In October of '67, Colonel White was reassigned to Saigon to become the Director of Operations for all Out-Of-Country missions. He was the first director to have ever flown in the North and that, along with his excellent other qualifications, made him the best man for the job. All of us who flew in North Vietnam really needed someone who could walk and chew gum without gagging in that shop. We needed all the help we could get and Colonel White promised to be an absolute treasure. The only problem was that he needed an Electronic Weapons Officer (EWO) in his shop and wanted Carlo. Carlo Lombardo was easily the best choice for the job, but it would break up our team and I was selfish enough to want to keep him. Colonel White actually asked me, a lowly Captain, if he could take Carlo. I was forced to smile and be a nice boy. I became an instant Strike Pilot and also 'D' Flight Commander instead of 'E' Flight, Weasel Commander.

Colonel White took me in to see our Wing Commander, Colonel Giraudo, who had replaced Colonel Scott in the summer. Colonel Giraudo, AKA the Great Kahuna, reluctantly agreed to let me finish out my remaining 60 missions for the magic 200. Carl Richter had been killed recently with only a couple to go for 200 and the all of the Brass were a bit nervous about allowing anyone to try for the 200 mark. I would rather have been a Weasel; however, captains take what they can get. I took over 'D' flight and started to relearn how to lead a Strike Flight. I flew my first Strike Flight Lead to Kep Airfield and my second to Phuc Yen. My third was to Kep again and I was back in the saddle. Three Route Pack six missions in three days are a good way to get back in shape.

I managed to slow myself down in the Takhli Stag Bar by dislocating my right shoulder while rolling for drinks. A 'Roll' consists of several staid, sober, careful folk looking at each other and yelling, "Last one with his feet on the bar-rail buys!" Everyone does a front roll and the last one to whack his feet on the bar rail buys a round for the mess. I tripped, dislocated my shoulder, AND had to buy for the bar. Not a very swift way to 'Roll" for drinks. Ted Moeller took me over to the Hospital and had my arm taped to my side for 10 days.

I spent the next fortnight being Supervisor of Flight (SOF), a job that ranks somewhere near dental work without anesthesia. I also heard a whole bunch of my "Friends" offer to 'Roll' for drinks. I finally got the shoulder working at about half speed and flew an Engine-Change test hop to prove I was ready and went back on the schedule.

One of the reasons I had been reassigned as a Strike Pilot was that all of the Squadrons were short of Mission Commanders. My Squadron, 357TFS, had only two, Lieutenant Colonel Tom Kirk, our boss, and Captain Neely Johnson. Neely and the Boss were both outstanding; however, we really needed at least 2 more to keep the workload down. While I was SOF for 10 days, Tom Kirk was shot down over Hanoi, not recovered, and Neely was the sole Mission Commander in the Squadron. I was scheduled to become a Mission Boss after my first 3 missions, but the dislocation put that on hold. I was scheduled for two more to see if the shoulder would work before I would be certified as a Mission Boss.

I led a flight to Kep the first day back and the next day, November 5, 1967; I led to Phuc Yen again. My call sign was Marlin and we were to be the last flight to roll in (Tail End Charlie). Flying a raid against Phuc Yen is about like being in hell with your back broke. The only thing worse is to be Tail End Charlie at Phuc Yen. The bad guys kept all of their MIG-21s there and objected rather firmly when we hit the Airfield. As I remember, there were over 1000 37mm and larger guns surrounding the place and it was covered by between 6 and 16 SAM Sites. Not exactly the best spot for a sight seeing trip.

The briefing for Marlin flight was a bit different on that day because I was checking out Major Frank Billingsley as an element lead. Frank was over 40, had come to the F-105 from C-141's, and had never flown any single-seat aircraft since he went through pilot training. Frank had been one of our students at McConnell and I had given him a couple of check flights before I went to Weasel School. He asked me to cover Rescue Procedures (RESCAP) during the mission briefing at the squadron. I asked why and he told me that if he were to really be an element lead, he might have to run a RESCAP. I told him that I would run the RESCAP if required. He said, "Not if you're the one on the ground" I covered RESCAP for at least 15 minutes and asked for questions. There were none and we suited up.

All of the ground routine went smoothly. Taxi, Takeoff, Join-up, Refueling, Pod Formation, and all of the other aspects of an RP-6 mission were routine. The Strike Force held a good Pod Position as we made our way through Laos and North Vietnam to the Red River crossing point about 10 miles downstream from Yen Bai. From there toward Phuc Yen the Strike Force flew at about 6,000 feet and 540 knots until we neared the MIG base and started our afterburner climb to roll-in altitude. For some reason the 3rd flight hung it high and waited way too long to start their attack which caused Marlin to be almost at 18,000 before we could head down the slide.

Our attack heading was almost east instead of southwest because of the delay and it seemed as though it took a week to fly down to release altitude of 7,000. Since our target was the last standing hangar on the airfield, it was easy to spot. The normal problems caused by the flack bursting in layers caused us to lose sight of the hangar two or three times, but it didn't move and was there when we got to our release parameters of 7,000', 45 degree dive, and 540 knots. The pass looked good at the time and, the next day when I saw the Bomb Damage Photos (BDA) we had put 18 of our 24 M-117 750# bombs through where the roof had been. Not too shabby for manual bombing.

I reefed my bird hard up and left at 5+ 'G' and did my normal roll right and then left to allow my wingmen to see me for the rejoin. Our problem was that we were now headed almost directly toward Hanoi and really had few options to avoid the vast amount of flack. I took the easiest way out by flying a loose left, jinking turn around Phuc Yen in order to fly on the north side of the complex and head for Thud Ridge. There were fewer guns on the north side. It took over a minute to rejoin. Before the flight could get into Pod Formation for SAM protection, we had 3 missiles launched at us from our six o'clock.

My choices were not very good. I could turn right and over-fly the north railroad and dodge the missiles while in the flack from the rail lines, I could turn left and fly back over Phuc Yen dodging missiles in even worse flack, or I could put the flight down in the weeds supersonic and haul for the ridge below 50'. I chose to mow the grass. Red-Dog, the Weasel flight, called the launch and told me which SAM site it was from. I jerked the bird around enough to catch sight of the first SA-2 Guideline missile and watched it hit the deck. My wingmen were almost in formation by now as I saw the second missile loose guidance commands and go up out of sight. At about the time I heard Red-Dog #3 call that he was hit and burning, I caught sight of the 3rd missile as it went into some houses and exploded. I decided to come up out of the grass and started a climb as Marlin Flight got into good Pod formation. We were at 750 knots and were below 100' above the rice paddies as I came out of after burner and continued to climb. As I passed through about 100' altitude, I saw several rounds zip by me and three hit my aircraft. I took three 57mm hits almost simultaneously. The rounds came from a 57mm site almost a mile north of us and were optically fired. These were the same guns that had hit Red-Dog. One round hit the afterburner section just above the right slab, one was in the bomb bay directly under my feet, and one was in the Air Turbine Motor (ATM) compartment just in front of my right knee. I kept in the climb at near military power and the cockpit instantly filled with smoke. I heard Red-Dog #3 calling that he was on fire and also heard his element lead tell him that he was in 'Great Shape', a big fat lie.

Red-Dog Three, Dutton and Cobiel bailed out over a rail yard less than 20 miles away and were put in the Hilton. Dick made it out in '73; however, Ed Cobiel died from torture he received from Fidel, the Cuban torture specialist at the Hilton.

I couldn't see anything because of the smoke and decided to blow the canopy. I flat could not find the canopy ejection handle on the left console and pulled some knob off trying, so, I flipped the manual canopy unlock lever under the canopy rail and the canopy went like it had been blown off. I was now in a convertible at 695 knots, still supersonic, climbing through 300'. I got two or three radio transmissions out before the radio died and every thing else decided to quit. It was probably a good thing the radio failed or everyone could have heard me squealing. The fire from the AB section caused the Fire and Overheat Lights to both come on and then quit. I checked the circuits and they didn't test (just like the good book says can happen when a big fire is on board). All three hydraulic gauges started down, bounced a few times, the utility gauge went to zero followed by primary flight gauge #2 (P2). PI (primary Flight#1) went slowly down and then dropped to zero. The oil pressure gauge went to visit the hydraulic gauges and every light on the peek and panic panel came on and then all of them quit. Shortly after the radio quit, I had a complete electrical failure followed by the failure of all pitot static flight instruments. The only thing in my Thud what worked was the Whiskey Compass and I think it was leaking alcohol.

I was still flying and heading up Thud Ridge away from Hanoi. I still had smoke coming into the cockpit and swirling around before the truly tremendous slipstream sucked it out. I caught myself reaching up and fanning the compass mounted on the canopy to see what heading I had. Now that is very stupid. I am in a 450-knot convertible fanning a compass. If my arm had gotten caught, I would have been sans arm. I started to laugh at my stupidity until I noticed that the right front quarter panel of the windscreen was starting to melt. I reached as far forward as I could and felt extreme heat from the fire in the ATM compartment. I am sure that the utility hydraulic reservoir had ruptured and was burning. The right quarter panel melted almost completely and shortly thereafter the right rudder pedal collapsed and dangled from the cables. I was now over half way up Thud Ridge and had turned for the Red River crossing. That was pure reflex, I guess. I then had an explosion in the Bomb bay, which blew the doors off and a small amount of fire came into the cockpit below my left foot. I had to hold my left foot up to stay clear of the flame. It wasn't all that hot due to the suction from the canopy area.

I had a couple more minutes to get to the river. I held what I had, trying to be the smoothest pilot in the world since I didn't have the foggiest how much hydraulic fluid I had in P2. The fire burned up from the AB section and the Aft Fuel Tank blew leaving only the aircraft ribs showing. The fire also burned up the right side of the aircraft, out into the right wing and the right main tire blew causing the right main to smack down into the slipstream and be ripped off the aircraft. All three of my wingmen looked like the Thunderbirds at an Academy Graduation. I had no right rudder pedal, no right gear strut, my bomb bay doors were missing, no lid on my cockpit, a melted hole in the windscreen, my left foot up, sundry other things disastrously wrong, BUT, I was coming up on the Red River. I found out afterwards that I had been called out as a SAM twice by other aircraft as I burned my way up the ridge. Marlin Three only said, "That's no Sam, that's Sparky" I started to think I had it made until the controls went and I became a passenger.

I still had 5 miles or so to go to cross the river when all of the controls went south. The bird pitched up, shuddered, rolled right like it was going to spin, and the started another pull-up. It was still going my way, so I held on to the stick to keep my arms from getting outside and stayed with my Thud. It would pull up sharply, shudder, shake, and snap right as if it were going to spin, and then start another pull-up. It did this three times until I was over the Red River. The last time it did snap into an inverted spin entry and I decided that it had taken me as far as it could go and pulled the handles up and squeezed the triggers. Only an F-105 could have taken that amount of punishment for 7 ½ minutes and deliver the driver to the river.

I still had one of my wingmen trying to fly formation and saw him flash by as I ejected. I had no idea what my altitude, airspeed, or attitude was since nothing worked except the Whiskey Compass. I learned that I was at 24,000', 270 knots and entering an inverted spin, BUT I was over the Red River. Being over the river was wonderful since the Rescue Jolly Green Giants were not allowed to cross the Red River for a rescue.

I fell about a week subjective time waiting for the 'chute to open at 10,000' and remembered that the last time I had ejected I had caught the risers under my chin and really put a Raspberry on my neck. I was at least not going to do that again. I stabilized on my back in a head down position that didn't spin and when I heard the spring motor in the parachute whir, I snapped my chin down just in time to catch the risers under it. I put another Raspberry on my neck.

When I looked down I was not quite across the river, so I hauled on the front risers and slipped across. I then saw that I was going to land near a small group of houses, so I went back up the risers and turned the 'chute and headed down stream. I pulled the front risers down and then got my knee in the riser 'Y' and did front riser slips to put as much distance between me and the houses until I was at about 200 feet or so above the jungle. I had come almost 4 miles and had two ridgelines between me and the nearest house or road. I looked down and decided that I needed to stop the slip and land in what I thought was 'Elephant Grass'. I landed in 75' tall bamboo.

I smashed into the bamboo and the 'chute caught with me at least 40 feet up. The bamboo broke and I fell the last 40 feet and landed like a sack of feed on a fairly steep hillside with no place to do any kind of a parachute landing fall (PLF). I didn't even do a Fighter Pilot PLF of heels, ass, and head; instead I just crumpled into a mound of goo. I broke my right patella, chipped a bone in my right elbow, dislocated my right shoulder again, had hairline fractures in several small bones in both feet, and landed on the family jewels with a mighty thump. I was down and across the river.

I moaned some, cursed even more, and managed to get the beeper from my parachute and shut it off. I pulled out my primary survival radio and found that the radios were very weak. Not to worry, I had two survival radios, three sets of batteries, the 'chute beeper and a partridge in a pear tree. I drank for one of my 6 baby bottles, contacted Frank Billingsley who was running the RESCAP in an exemplary fashion, and started to move down the hill and find a place I could see the sky.

If you have never been in bamboo, don't go. It is not a nice place. I would end up several feet in the air trying to squeeze through the bamboo and have to break my way back down. I moved about 200 yards in about 15 minutes and worked my way into 25 foot tall ferns that made the bamboo look like a good place. It took another 10 or so minutes to wiggle out of the fern thicket and get under a huge tree. I tried to find a better place and gave up since the whole area was bamboo and/or ferns. I talked to Frank and vectored him into my tree and asked him to check his fuel. He in informed me that he was running this show and to shut up. He also told me that he had a better view than I did, had sent the wingmen out for fuel, and was about to have to leave for a while. I found out that he left my tree, 75 miles northwest of Hanoi, with less than 2000 pounds of fuel. He went to a tanker and was back in 29 minutes. The tanker could not have been in Laos. Everyone was trying his best to pick my worthless butt up.

I sat under my tree for almost 20 minutes; it seemed like a week, until I heard a burner light. I came up on the survival radio and had a call from Ozark; a flight of four from Korat who had my cap until Frank got back. I vectored them into my tree and they set up a cap away from me to keep the bad guys guessing. Frank called back a few minutes later with the rest of Marlin Flight and took back the RESCAP duties. I was starting to get lonely and had finished two of my baby bottles when Frank told me that the Sandies were inbound. I had been on the ground for only a bit over 2 hours clock time or a month subjective time. I started to believe I had a chance. I inventoried my stuff and put everything I was going to take out away. Pistols, spare radio and batteries, the beeper, all seven knives I carried, my Medical kit, and my trade goods kit. I kept out several flares and two pen-gun flare kits.

The Sandies called shortly thereafter, at about 1630 local time, and I managed to vector them into my tree. They left to set up an orbit away from me and I waited very anxiously for the HH-3 to arrive. I listened to the Jolly call in and then all hell seemed to break loose. Some MIG-17's showed up and the Sandies became most nervous. The Jolly tried to calm things down and the Low Sandy came by to mark my position with a Willy Pete (White Phosphorous) Bomb. The Sandy then marked another location for some reason and The Low Jolly went there. I had 17 aircraft in my CAP and everyone started to talk at once. The Jolly went to the wrong place and then headed back to me. All this time I could see a little patch of sky only about 30 feet in diameter. Frank made a pass at the Low Jolly and turned him towards me and shouted for me to, "Do something!" I pulled out my pen-gun flare and fired and reloaded as fast as possible. I bounced a flare off his canopy and saw the pilot jump and then hover in my tree.

The Radio went absolutely Able Sugar with people shouting out MIG calls and as I watched the penetrator come down towards me. I had stowed my radio and did not hear a transmission from Harry Walker who was told that there were MIGs in the area. His answer was, "Keep them off my ass, I've got better things to do!" and stayed in the hover with his rotor blades whacking the tree well below the top. I backed out to see the cable operator, but the open space was so small I couldn't see squat. The cable stopped a few feet above me and then came down some more and was level with me a bit down a steep slope.

I couldn't jump because of my ankles and knee and then it swung towards me and I let it hit the ground and discharge a huge spark. I then unzipped the straps, pulled down on the folding seat, put my legs around the penetrator, really tightened the straps around my body, and yanked on the cable as hard as I could. I was pulled off the ground and up about 50 feet or so.

The HH-3E pivoted 180 degrees and started to pull me up and through the tree as it accelerated to his max speed. It was a very wild ride for a while. I broke out of the canopy at top speed for the Jolly as the winch hauled me up. The door gunner was firing his mini gun at something; so, I whipped out my 38 and shot the jungle. I figured I could get off six rounds and make everything lighter.

I was pulled in the door and hugged by the crew. I thought I would be the happiest man in the world, but the crew of Harry Walker's HH-3E were happier than I was. The whole crew was laughing like mad, so I asked what was funny and was told that Harry had just said," Tell the SOB not to die until we get him to a hospital. We need a live one for a change." It seems they had picked up two guys who were dead in the last six weeks. I had problems standing and the Paramedic (PJ) sat me down and started to check me out.

The first thing he did was to strap a parachute on me. I sure as hell didn't want to use one of those again for a while. He asked if I was hurt and I told him I had some small problems. He them put me on a stretcher and gave me a good once over. It was noisy as all hell in the Jolly and since I didn't have a headset I had real problems hearing. He pulled out a Morphine Styrete case and I said NO. He grinned and showed me a miniature of Jack Daniel's Black Label that was in the tube. It was exactly what the doctor ordered.

I guess I was beat up worse than I thought since I went into shock for a while. The whole crew took off their jackets and piled them around me to keep me warm. I straightened out in time to watch the Jolly refuel on the way back. The PJ and the flight engineer helped me up to the cockpit and I sat on the jump seat as the C-130 came over us, stopped just in front and then let down until the hose was only 50 feet or so in front. We were in Laos with all of the Low Level Fuel Lights on just after sunset. There were layered clouds that were black with a blood red sun shining from below up through and between them. It was incredible. Harry moved the big HH-3E up to the hose, stuck it, and took gas. It was all very smooth, very easy, and very beautiful. I was the second furthest north rescue in the whole war. The whole crew of very brave men had risked their lives to pull me from the jungle. Henry did understand what 'We Band Of Brothers' meant.

We went to Nakon Phanom (NKP), AKA Naked Fanny, and landed about 2100 hours. I was on a stretcher and really couldn't walk. I was treated like the crown jewels and rushed to the hospital for a check up. I was on the x-ray machine that was broken when Brigadier General McBride came in. Willy P. had been my Wing Commander at Spangdahlem and was a very nice and very funny man. He went into a routine about having given me a perfectly good F-105 and I had dumped it! He was not going to give me any more. He also brought a bottle of Old Overshoes Rye Mission Whiskey and a six-pack of warm Millers beer. We both sat on the x-ray and drank the Old Overshoes neat with warm beer chaser. He also told me that The Great Kahuna had sent the Takhli Gooney Bird for me and it was inbound.

I was taken from the Hospital, never having seen a Doctor, and loaded on the C-47 in my stretcher. When we were airborne, the pilot came back and put my going home ration from Colonel Giraudo on my chest, a bottle of Chivas Regal, a glass, and a bucket of ice. The Chivas was to get me back to Takhli in good humor. It did a very good job. When we landed the crew turned the stretcher so I could see what was happening. I was met by the fire suppression helicopter, fire trucks, over 1000 folk, and was treated to a Hundred Mission Parade at near midnight Takhli time.

When we stopped, the doors of the Gooney Bird swung open and The Great Kahuna jumped into the C-47 and hollered, "Throw her up!" A very shapely female flew through the air and landed in Colonel Giraudo's arms. He came over, dumped her on me and said, "Welcome Home Sparky, look what I brung ya!" The lady, Vicky Nixon, had just arrived that day and was the first female on the base. She was his brand new secretary, very sharp, and she was scared spitless. I was laughing like a hyena and decided to try and calm her down since she was actually shaking. I whispered in her ear, "I just fell out of a tree, landed on my jewels, and there isn't a thing I could do to you!" She looked at me, started to cry, really hugged me, and said, "You poor baby!" We were placed in the back of Colonels 'G's pickup, still on my stretcher, and given a tour of the base. Neely Johnson who I was supposed to relieve as a Force Commander met me with the Flight Commanders for the morning go and saluted me from the C-47.

I was grounded and that was my last combat mission. I tried to talk the Boss out of his decision, but I went home. I was the first guy from Takhli that was picked up from North Vietnam in over eleven months that made it back to Takhli. Frank Billingsley did a perfect job the first time he ran a RESCAP and I am the most fortunate person in the world. I never did get to help Neely out. He finished his tour after having led over one third of his total missions into Route Package Six.

PERSONAL REFLECTION
RITA KAY WHITTINGHILL

The single supreme moment in my life was meeting Dell Whittinghill. She was the 8th of 9 children of Emmett Whittinghill and Ruth Celeste Whittinghill, nee Smithers, born on the Vernal Equinox in 1936. Dell described her parents as 'Passionate Protestants'. Named Rita Kay, but became 'Dell' because a Paternal Aunt, May Gandin, was childless and had always wanted a daughter named Dell. Her parents moved from Owensboro Kentucky to New Albany Indiana during the depression seeking a better life. New Albany was marginally better than in Kentucky, but was likewise no box of chocolates. There were six girls and three boys in her family, and they all felt the pinch of poverty. The girls did well at school, were all pretty and intelligent, and had successful marriages. Feelings immediately informed me that Dell was the best of all the Whittinghill girls. The Whittinghill boys didn't flourish. Father Whittinghill was a severe man not easily forthcoming with praise, especially regarding his sons. Dell's mother, Ruth, was altogether different. A bit over 5' she had a naturally sweet disposition. I never heard a cross word from her. When Dell was in Junior High, the family had a house near the High School and had also managed to buy a small place southeast of New Albany off the River Road. It even had room for a big garden. By the time I met Dell, they had built a small house there, only she and her younger sister, Evelyn, were still at home.

The first time I saw Dell was after a basketball game, after playing a Sax Solo at half time with the pep band. She failed to swoon, but finally agreed to go out with me that night. A few times after that I walked her to the bus station - but the first time we danced was at the "C's, a Catholic Teen Club where you could also 'hang out' and meet people. Unfortunately, it was well chaperoned. I was a junior at New Albany High (NAHS) and Dell was a sophomore. She was the first younger girl I had found interesting. I hadn't found any 'young chicks' that struck me as worth pursuing, but Dell stood out. We only went out a few times before my best friend, Reid Crosby, latched onto her - and suddenly she became 'Reid's Girl.' I dated around after that but never got serious with anyone. If they could dance and laugh, I told myself that was reason enough to be happy. I did a lot of double-dating with Crosby and Dell, and got more impressed with her - but it wasn't reciprocal. She thought me a clown too big for my britches. From time to time he would make her angry and I got to be the patsy who 'fixed' things up. This melodrama went on for quite a while. Reid graduated in '51, and since Alumni could not go to Proms, he asked me to take Dell to my senior (her junior) Prom. I happily agreed, and we had a tremendous ball on the 'Belle of Louisville,' a Stern-wheel Steamboat right out of Mark Twain. I did as I was asked, kept her out all night, and even took her to school next morning in her Prom dress. After that, I mentioned to Reid that he better get another patsy because she was looking finer all the time.

Reid and I went to Indiana U. together the next fall and I seldom saw Dell until the summer break. That summer that went bust because every place in the Ohio Valley was on strike, and it meant neither Reid nor I could go back to IU in the fall. Crosby continued to periodically make Dell mad and break off their relationship. My usual job was to get her to reconsider and make nice. I told Crosby that all bets were now off, and next time I'd be chasing Ms. Dell.

Since there was no work anywhere, we spent the summer of '53 goofing off. Reid soon volunteered for the draft and went to Wurzburg, Germany, assigned to an Army Band. I held the dogs at bay by digging ditches until September when I got a real job as a Ballistic Tech at the DuPont Powder Plant in Charleston, Indiana. Reid finally goofed-up one time too many, and I began pursuing Dell. Crosby told me that, *if* I could catch her, to wait until he got back to be our best man.

Because I was running around like a nut, establishing beer drinking records, and performing the fifties teen version of 'way cool,' Dell unaccountably remained less than charmed. She graduated, moved away from home and went to work for Bell Telephone in Louisville. After I started at DuPont, I began a campaign plan to change her mind. We danced, dined, had long philosophical conversations - and she started to believe I might actually be a person. By spring she decided to like me a lot and accepted my Fraternity Pin, but said she would only marry me after I graduated, finished my stint in the Service, and 'settled myself.' That sounded like about six years, and I was definitely thinking 'sooner.' I deftly kept up my subtle pressure. By the time I returned to IU in 54, Dell was 'My Girl' and fiancé. I continued working on the remaining problem that year and successfully got her to add lust to being in love. Passion then slid our six-year goal up a bit to July 16, 1955, and Crosby stood there as our best man. I congratulated myself a lot.

Dell and I traveled to IU that fall in a tiny vintage trailer, and she put her life entirely on hold for me. She worked at Bell, paid the bills, and I was the student. A woman who would do that for anyone has already shown the man that he's as lucky as he can ever get. In that and other ways, Dell is the most special person I've ever met. I generally tell her that I married her because of her cutest derriere in the known universe - although the rest of her is also generously easy on the eyes.

The deciding reason was her character. She has extraordinary integrity. She is, as well, an admirably gentle person - with a steel backbone when needed.

She has stayed right with me through genuinely bad times and always supported me. She can also snap me to serious attention when that's needed. She held our finances together when I was gone for long periods. She raised our children almost entirely by herself - again, because of my absence almost all of the time. She made me feel like a champ even when I struggled to keep my head up. She is yet the best dancer I ever held in my arms, skies far better than I, and remains fearless when she must be - all after more than fifty years of marriage. I may be a better pilot, but I'm convinced that's only because she never tried it. Few people are as fortunate as I. My greatest hope is that she truly knows how deeply I feel that she is the finest blessing to ever happen to me.

11014222R00147

Made in the USA
San Bernardino, CA
03 May 2014